The Principal: Traversing the High-Wire with No Net Below

79 Places Where the High-Wire Can Be Greasy

by

Dr. Don Sternberg

RoseDog❧Books

PITTSBURGH, PENNSYLVANIA 15222

RoseDog Books
701 Smithfield Street
Pittsburgh, PA 15222
Visit our website at *www.rosedogbookstore.com*

ISBN: 978-1-4349-3108-5
eISBN: 978-1-4349-7176-0

The Principal: Traversing the High-Wire with No Net Below

79 Places Where the High-Wire Can Be Greasy

Don Sternberg, Ed.D.

<u>Dedication</u>

Dedicated to my wife Kathy, our children Elyssa and Adam, and to all present and future principals who have the courage to step out onto the high-wire and make a difference for students.

About the Author

Recognized as New York State's 2009 Principal of the Year, by the National Association of Elementary Principals and by Redbook magazine for leading one of the 72 best elementary schools in the United States, Don Sternberg knows what it takes to walk the high-wire that an elementary school principal faces every day. His 42-plus year career in the public education, as a teacher, assistant principal, principal, college instructor, as well as recognition by peers for his outstanding performance gives Don expertise and credibility that few can match. In <u>The Principal: Traversing the High-Wire with No Net Below</u>, he shares his insights about how to successfully lead within the public education arena keeping the most important constituency, the students, front and center in all he does.

The 735 students that count on Don to create an environment that ignites their learning is Don's inspiration. He navigates the often competing constituencies of teachers, parents, unions, administration and outside interests with rare grace that embodies what most parents hope for in their children's principals. Outside of his duties, Don serves as a co-president of the Nassau County Elementary School Principals' Association and is a member of the Long Island School Leadership Advisory Council. He is also a certified assessor as part of the National Association of Secondary School Principals, Selecting and Developing 21st Century Principals Initiative and has served on the New York State Educational Leadership Assessment Content Advisory Committee.

Don is adjunct lecturer in educational administration at the State University of New York at Stony Brook and an instructor at a number of online universities. His writing has appeared in *Principal* magazine as well as the *School Administrators Association of New York State Journal*. He is also a member of the Editorial Advisory Board for the National Association of Elementary School Principals. Don's doctoral studies in educational administration from Columbia University focused on the effectiveness of early intervention programs. In addition to his doctorate, he holds a masters degree in educational administration from Long Island University and a masters in fine arts from Adelphi University. His undergraduate degree is from Ball State University in Muncie, Indiana.

Contents

The Principal: Traversing the High-Wire with No Net Below
79 Places Where the High-Wire May Be Greasy

Introduction

"If you want to build a ship, don't herd people together to collect wood and don't be so rigid to assign tasks and work, but rather teach them to long for the immensity of the sea" -Antoine de Saint-Exupery

As a school principal, I have strong feelings about that passage in conjunction with getting *all* of the stakeholders in a school to see the big picture: building a program that educates, supports, inspires, and motivates children to learn. All effective long-term plans are strategic, and their operational segments must remain focused on the long-term goal and potential outcome. All too often, principals try to manage competing objectives, and those objectives are not synchronized into a tapestry that helps to bring to fruition the *big picture*. The orchestration of the big picture is an enterprise that involves and requires the engagement of all stakeholders associated with your school. Moving that process forward in a steady, positive and unencumbered fashion will be your job as principal. You probably know how to theoretically accomplish this task. The question is can you do it for real – on the job – in the heat of the moment – when one false move could have drastic consequences?

The minefield that is public school administration is littered with the bleached bones of both new and established principals who could not successfully traverse the period between their first day as a principal to their retirement party. During that time, you will be a *high-wire aerialist*, traversing the wire from the beginning of your career, as you step off the platform and onto the wire-high above the ground, until you step off the wire at the other end and onto the platform that is retirement. All eyes will be cast upward toward you. As you place one foot in front of another you are, in most cases and in most situations, *alone*. At times, as principal, you can feel that you are a hundred feet off the ground, traversing your career alone – spotlight beaming up at you – and with no net under you. As you look at the long, thin strand of wire ahead of you, *is that grease you see and who the hell put that there?*

Regardless of the network of colleagues: educational stakeholders associated with your building, the department chairs, area directors, lead teachers, assistant principals – you name it - the bottom line is that you are the principal, *and there is only one principal!* Hence, the sense that at times you are crossing a hire-wire above everything and everyone, with everyone watching your *every* move and with your *every* move having an impact. And, did I mention the glare of the spotlight! There will be constant stakeholder judgment of whether you are doing things correctly and people looking in judgment at your *every* decision and your *every* step.

As if the responsibilities of being a principal were not difficult enough, there are places on your high-wire that are *potentially* greasy. While some of these slippery spots are just the nature of the job with all the ramifications of being a leader and a decision maker, other spots may be the result of *your actions and/or inactions.* Yes, *you* may actually be greasing *your own* high-wire!

Knowing where the wire *can be* potentially more dangerous is important! You are attempting to move forward, one precarious step at a time; eyes focused ahead, never down, never to the side and never back. Having an understanding of where the high-wire is potentially greased is extremely important, so you can get yourself successfully through those areas. It is just as important to be mindful of how you could prevent adding grease to your own high-wire because obviously, you do not want to be your own worst enemy. Knowing where the high-wire is greased will allow you to successfully grow old on the high-wire. Now the word *successful* can have a variety of meanings depending on your perspective. Success can simply mean *making it* to retirement. However, success can also mean (and should mean) facilitating the creation of a school that fully supports student learning and teacher growth. You choose. It is your career; *it is your high-wire.*

Remaining Balanced

Consider this book as the long balancing pole of your high-wire principalship. I want it to serve as a comfort and to support you to maintain your balance. Who knows, it may also serve as a roadmap. It is important for you to understand the series of interpersonal relationships with each stakeholder group (students, parents, teachers, building support staff, central office administration, fellow administrators, board of education members, and community leaders) will be what constitutes your route on the high-wire. Your failure to maintain a working relationship (your balance on the wire, so to speak) with *each* constituent group will eventually serve as the amount of grease on your high-wire.

Knowing where the wire is potentially greased, how it got greasy, or (as unthinkable as it might appear at first blush) *who* greased it, and how to get it ungreased are keys to your success. Your common sense and survival instincts, coupled with the knowledge that you will learn from my experiences will allow you to be around to pick up that gold watch or set of golf clubs from the faculty twenty or twenty-five years from now.

Leadership to me is the ability to get things accomplished in a successful manner and that is what this book is all about. You are on a course to build relationships and, at the same time, being weary of relationships. For in the end, it will be those relationships that will sustain your career or put an abrupt, quick slip and a long fall, end to it. *Did I mention that there is no net?*

The Walk from Theoretical to Practical

While much has been written on the concept of leadership in the past fifty years, it can be somewhat difficult to find compelling literature that is both *practical* and *clearly applicable* to *educational* leadership. It is not that there is a shortage of scholarly writings and research pertaining to educational leadership. Rather, the difficulty lies in having to sort through an abundance of theory (and *in theory* even Communism works) to find something that is relative and practical to enhance one's repertoire of leadership skills.

Donald G. Krause, in his book <u>The Art of War for Executives</u>, highlights the nature of being a leader and puts it best when he states, "Leadership comes from within ... [it's] grounded in character. Effective leadership is an aggregate of the character and......the effectiveness of organizational activities depends on the tone and quality of the character of its leaders" (Krause, 2005, p.31).

Leadership comes in layers and your actions and interactions with all stakeholders are performed in layers. They are built upon one another and are intertwined with each other. Leadership is also *always* a work - a layering - in progress and good leaders allow themselves to be a continuum of growth. You will probably never know enough or be able to do enough that will result in a plateau of perfection. Leadership is the ability to get things accomplished in a successful manner and that means *minimizing* or *totally avoiding* the grease spots. And that is what this book is all about, helping you see some *potential* slippery spots as you make your way through your career. From observations and discussions with colleagues during the past four decades, it is apparent that these grease spots are quite universal!

You may look at a new principal just like a new minted teacher. If you observe both you can see a pattern of the same mistakes. There can be a lack of self-confidence. There can be an assumption that something complex is simple and that something that is simple *has to become* complex. If talented, people grow out of and learn from these mistakes, *in time*. The significant difference is that no one expects very much from a first year teacher. However, a first year principal has a tumultuous set of demands on them coming from all directions and the expectations set the high-wire *very* high.

Chapter 1

I do firmly believe that leadership comes from how you see yourself and others see you. I am naturally an *introvert* and I am amazed when I see others performing the science and art of teaching. I believe that is what makes me an effective leader. I *highly respect* educators who can walk into a classroom filled with twenty-five to thirty students and captivate them with their knowledge and skill. The process (art and science) of *effective* teaching is something that not everyone can do. My respect for outstanding educators will not allow me to be anything but a participatory/servant leader. I do not buy into the bees and honey thing as a leader. I believe you attract people by the way you show respect for what they do. No one walks over me but I am well aware of the true pedagogical talent, knowledge, and skill when I see it, and I let those teachers *teach and lead.*

The Beach

Those first few steps out onto the high-wire as a principal can be scary but at that time in your career you may have the *temporary* safety net of a honeymoon period. Honeymoons can be sweet and comfortable, a period in time of mutual discovery and where much can be forgiven. You are learning about your faculty and staff as well as the other stakeholder groups associated with your school, as they are, in turn, learning about you. Those first few steps out onto the high-wire appear to be warm, comforting, and well-supported by all those around you. As a realistic aerialist, though, you must constantly be aware that you cannot make your reputation in one day but you can lose it in a day! Your immediate thought might be that these initial steps onto the high-wire could *never* be greased – or could it! As you enter your new surroundings, the *wise* rookie or *wryly* veteran of other schools always listens twice as often as they speak. Wishful thinkers may believe these initial easy steps will define the entire walk, but in new surroundings, with expectations high, the realist knows better.

The Two Ears, One Mouth Ratio

All of us are provided with, as standard equipment, two ears and one mouth. One of the tenets of strong relationship building is the use of this equipment in the ratio that it was provided to you. Leaders who have strong and effective relationships *listen to* their stakeholders *sans* interrupting or pre-judging what they think the other person is going to say. The best leaders have developed the intuitiveness to also *listen beyond the words* to hear the real message. The practice of *deliberate inquiry* allows for the candid exchange of ideas, concepts, and fosters and supports initiatives. Projects get off the ground smoothly and with a greater degree of potential positive fruition when the construct is based upon strong partnerships formed by clear understandings.

Listening has never been at the forefront of administrative theory. There are no courses devoted to the *practice and art of listening* and maybe there should but perhaps it is something only developed through keeping your mouth closed and ears open! Men, your wife or significant other will probably insist that you never listen and women, your husband or significant other will say that you listen (and remember) too much. Sometimes all a teacher, student, or a parent of a child wants is to be heard. Teachers need to feel they are a participant in the decision-making of the school via your *ears*, heart, and mind. They need to feel that their opinions are valued and credibly utilized in the decisions or choices that only you can make. A good leader encourages active participation of all the staff members. When everyone is on the same page, it makes for an effective learning environment. Being on the same page doesn't simplistically mean that everyone agrees with everything and/or everyone else. Being on the same page simply means that there is an agreement on what the issues and/or initiatives are and the processes by which the situations/initiatives will be addressed. It means that there is consensus on how the situations/initiatives will be introduced and how assessments will be conducted. *Consensus doesn't happen unless everyone is listening.*

Effective leadership is derived not from power and authority, but on operating principles that the staff sees in your actions and can sense from your relationship skills. It requires the confidence to let people discuss solutions to problems without telling them how to solve problems. Leadership means recognizing that those talented people who work for the same school you are leading have the same goals you have.

The key to successful relationships with people is the mindfulness to be respectful and caring of individuals, regardless of your differences. Build relationships with all of the school's stakeholders to garner their support and respect the fact that they have individual opinions, strengths, circumstances, and weaknesses. I submit to you that the power of all of the above starts with you being an *outstanding* listener. And as someone new to a school, it will be all about building relationships and, at this time at least, listening more than speaking. Failure to do so is the *first* [**Grease Spot #1**] potential grease-spot on your high-wire.

Beach Building Basics

I have always related success as a principal with building a beach. From the first day you are principal, to the day when you leave the building for the last time, you are constructing that beach and painstakingly - literally, one grain of sand at a time. Your beach must be constructed one grain of sand at a time because sustainable relationships within organizations are built that way - one person at a time - one action or reaction at a time.

It takes time to build sustainable relationships across the wide spectrum of people connected with a school. There are many interest groups that a principal must work with and, at times, there are conflicting desires on the part of individual stakeholder groups. Create relationships that are built on integrity, trust, and credibility, and slowly even the most polarized of positions held by opposing groups have the best chance of being reasonably resolved. Being *caught* between opposing groups can become a significant supplier of grease [**Grease Spot #2**] to your high-wire.

The last thing anyone wants to hear is a principal standing in front of a large gathering of school stakeholders and *asking* the group to trust him or her. Asking for trust won't get it! Certain powers accrue to the position, but they are derived from what the constituents have conferred and will allow. What people do want is to work with a principal who can be trusted day in and day out, and whose credibility and integrity are never in question. The establishment of that kind of relationship does not happen overnight, but rather is built at the pace of one grain of sand at a time.

There is a duality to a principal's role. On the one hand, he or she must align all stakeholders towards a unified organizational culture and purpose. On the other hand, he or she must rely on the input from dozens of individuals on a daily basis, even though many of those individuals may be in conflict with one another. The single, unifying role of a trusted and credible principal is that he or she assists in bringing these potentially conflicting parties together.

You cannot rely on a huge amount of sand dumped onto your beach at one time. You cannot expect a faculty to immediately have a relationship with the new principal who stands up in front of them on day one and says, "Trust me, I am here for you and to assist you in building a great school." What if the faculty already thinks it is a great school? What are they then thinking that you are thinking about them? What if you are the third principal that they have heard this from in the last five years? Initially, saying very little can be the best advice, as you enter an environment that you really know very little about. You are certainly granted a place to construct your beach during the honeymoon period. However, that foundation will not sustain you and that foundation will not last unless it is augmented with additional sand. So, how do you build your beach? How do you start the process and get into the rhythm of one grain after another after another and so on and on and on?

The level of beach building commitment that most new principals and even veterans do not want to hear about is that even after over three decades as a principal, I am *still* building my beach. Every constructive thing I do, every day, is a beach building activity, and an additional grain of sand on my beach. Because the fact of the matter is that your beach will be naturally eroded from time to time and, hopefully, as a continuing learner, you are always growing, *always* learning ways of adding more sand.

Every time you return a phone call within a reasonable amount of time (or sooner), every time you make a teacher's, student's, or a parent's priority your priority, you add a grain of sand to your beach. Every time you stop and listen when a teacher asks, "Do you have a minute?" and every time you illustrate through action and deed that teachers should have a huge involvement in deciding how best to educate kids; what resources and materials should be available and what is working and what is not; you are adding a grain of sand. Lest you think a new principal must do everything someone asks them to do, I suggest that you read on because that is not the case. And there is certainly a way to say *no*, that can also, surprisingly, add sand to your beach.

Add a Grain Here and There

You are walking down the hallway and some paper is scattered on the floor and you reach down and pick it up. What does that tell the custodian who happens to be behind you, down at the other end of the hallway, and sees you doing that? Well, one of two things. He or she will think that this person (you) thinks no job is beneath them, or they will file a grievance against you because you are working out of contract – although, it will probably be, I surmise, 99.99% the former! Think of the response from that custodian who sees you picking up paper in a hallway or grabbing a mop because water is racing out of a urinal or pulling out an overflowed garbage can in the cafeteria and re-placing it with an empty one. You are walking by the desk of your secretary and she is swamped with phones ringing and students and teachers waiting (some more patiently than others). What do you think your clerical staff will say when you start asking a couple of kids, "Can I help you?" Or, you ask a teacher waiting at the secretary's desk, "Helen, how can I help you?" What about jumping behind the food service counter on pizza day, when the kitchen staff is down a person, just to assist in getting the food out. Or, covering a class until a substitute can be located for a teacher who just got a call from her kid's school that there is an emergency and she has to rush there.

You cannot simply request being part of a team. You must *earn* a place on the team. You, as the new principal, will be given opportunities to become part of the team and you should also *look for ways* to be a teammate. Every time you do something like the above, you have placed a grain of sand on your beach. But what have you really done? You have acted as part of the team! No one is expecting you to be able to bend steel with your bare hands or turn water into wine – although, a little support from Dr. Merlot is always appreciated (but, please, wait until Friday after school).

Beach Erosion

There will be times when your beach will erode. A stormy situation will approach and when it has left, your beach will be *a little less* than it was prior to the storm. There is no way, during a career where each and every day you make decisions, that your beach will remain completely intact and/or pristine. It is what you do and how you handle yourself during these difficult, beach erosion times that will say more about you and your leadership abilities than when the sun is shining and everyone is sitting and eating Ben and Jerry's Cherry Garcia on *your* beach. Potentially, a greasy spot [**Grease Spot #3**] is your ability to take-on-water (have sand erode) and still remain calm, intelligent, logical, resourceful, and understanding. Remember, people will be watching you up there on your high-wire!

If beach erosion is the result of your mistake or an error in judgment, admit it and learn from it. I always tell the teachers new to the school that they will make a dozen mistakes and that is understandable. The only caveat here is that I don't want to see them making the *same* mistake a dozen times! I tell them that I want to know what happened, what they were thinking, and, most importantly, what did they learned from the experience. I apply the same questions to myself. As principal, having a clear and honest reflective practice will be a key way to support yourself (more about reflective practices later).

Finally, you have greased *your own high-wire* [**Grease Spot #4**] if you attempt to spin or cover up your action(s). People respect those who can admit an error and who can learn from it. You will be greatly surprised at how much sand is *not* removed when you own-up to a situation that probably could have been handled differently. In fact, it is my opinion that a few grains of sand are actually added when you admit your error.

5

Smile Power

One of the first things I learned as a new principal was that everyone is always looking at you and to you for a myriad of reasons. Regardless of whether or not I am having a good day or a bad day, my facial expression is as important to me and my position as it is to a great poker player. The concept of never forgetting that you are the boss and that people will always interested in your reaction to them is critically important.

As a principal, I have come to learn the power of the smile. I do not roam the hallways, classrooms, and general access areas of the school with a grim on my face somewhere between Batman's Joker and Alice in Wonderland's Cheshire Cat. Neither would be appropriate or effective. What I do postulate to you is the concept that you be aware of *who you are* in your professional world and realize that you are always *on*. A sullen or anger demeanor, as you traverse the rooms and hallways of your building, will have an impact and, I respectfully suggest, a poor one [**Grease Spot #5**].

It will be taken *personally* by all who see you because it will be internalized by each person that you are mad/upset with them and/or you think they did something wrong. I further hypothesize that this will be true for students as well as staff. A friendly hello, a warm good morning or good afternoon is a minor salutation and a gesture that is as important a component to your position as anything you initiate. Yes, there will be times that you are upset, displeased, and not a happy camper and no one can expect that you will be walking around like a Disney employee, however, being *on* is on and you will be *on* all the time - please do not forget it.

Building Relationships

Before you are a leader, success is all about growing yourself. When you become a leader, success is all about growing others. -Jack Welch

Leadership involves collaboration and successful leadership necessitates the building of *strong* relationships. The three cornerstones of any successful relationship are the establishment of *Integrity*, *Credibility*, and *Trust*. While leaders can make decisions solely based upon their authority, it is often times not the best methodology.

Integrity, Credibility, and Trust (ICT): The Best Grease Chasers

I have written about the concept of your high-wire and your ability to traverse the wire without finding yourself flat on your back and looking up at it. I hope I have been able to start to illustrate the effort it takes to maintain your position on your high-wire and make it to the other side as you traverse areas that could be slippery. How your action (or lack of action) creates the greased areas is up to you and how you traverse the areas greased by others are the skill sets that you will need to develop - *on the job training* - as you are on the wire itself. Nothing can *really* prepare you for the job except doing the job.

I would be significantly remiss if I did not write a few paragraphs about what your high-wire should be made of to support you during your journey from neophyte school building principal through many years of success and into retirement. Your high-wire, created by you, must be made of three strands woven together for purposes of strength and endurance. The three strands are *Integrity, Credibility, and Trust*.

You *cannot ask for* any of these three strands. They all *must be earned*. And, all three *must be* present to ensure the strength and durability of your high-wire. All three strands, I submit, are permanently woven together, and if just one of the three snaps, your effectiveness as a principal is *seriously* diminished [**Grease Spot #6**] and, for the most part, irreparable. In fact, it is irreparable to the degree that the only way to regain the component is to start fresh in a new school district.

You have to earn all three and there should be no expectation on your part of getting them all after one specific action, deed, time period or that you will be anointed with them. These three strands allow you to move forward and support your position as leader. Think about it, who doesn't want a leader who has *integrity*, is *credible* and can be *trusted*. The interesting part here is that you neither have nor do not have *Integrity, Credibility, and Trust* when you start as a new principal. You are a blank canvas! Your actions (or lack thereof) will provide the paint and brushes by which you will be painted by your stakeholders. Loyalty, commitment, energy and productivity are the direct result of a leader having *Integrity, Credibility, and Trust*.

Credibility means walking the talk. A teaching staff needs to see that the principal is not just full of lofty thoughts and statements. If you say you believe in safe and caring environments, take steps to create one. If you say you believe in building teacher capacity, build capacity. If you want collaborative teams, collaborate. If you want a learning culture, demonstrate *you* are learning. The list is endless and the perils of the high-wire are significant if you are just talk and no action. Everyone is watching what you do and say – it comes with the territory – and if you don't follow your words with actions, your *integrity, credibility, and the trust people put in you* will be gone.

My Schwinn

I lost my wallet once. I've lost the keys to my car twice. I lost my bicycle when I was seven years old and have misplaced and never found countless pairs of sunglasses, reading glasses and a Monte Blanc pen. Three things, however, I have *never* lost and protect almost as dearly as I protect my own kids: the *trust* others have in me and my *credibility and integrity*. Once lost, they will follow the pens, reading and sunglasses, my Schwinn, and the commemorative Monte Blanc pen that marked the earning of my doctorate - gone forever. *Integrity, credibility, and trust* are built slowly. No one is going to just give you their trust that would be earned based upon your integrity and credibility. The thing about integrity, credibility, and trust is that they really are an all or nothing proposition. You cannot have a little integrity or a little credibility or even a little trust, and you also *cannot* lose just a little of each.

So your high-wire balancing act is exacerbated by the fact that you are attempting to gain integrity, credibility, and trust by your actions and interactions with everyone and at the same time that you are trying not to lose any of it. Talk about a greasy stretch of your high-wire!

The warping of your integrity, credibility, and trust starts with *spinning*. Any great *master of spin* will indicate that what they said was not a lie but rather *a possible* misinterpretation by the listener. After all, a spin is not a lie - sort of; it is simply the spun truth. Spinning the truth is making what happened plausible by embellishing it, so spin is not a lie – really – it is simply truth with a spin on it. As you spin events, incidents, and interpretations of what occurred, all in your effort to save face, you start the *spin cycle*. Eventually, people will see the spin of your explanations and your credibility and integrity will be irreparably damaged. A small lie is a spin - seemingly hurting no one but rather an attempt on your part to save face but when uncovered there is no way to spin your way out and regain the same standing you once had. People want to be treated with respect. How do you think people will feel about you when they discover the spin that you placed on the last conversation that you had with them [**Grease Spot #7**]?

Credibility, trust, and integrity will buy you the entire run of the high-wire. It is what quality and effective leadership is built upon over time. When you are believed and trusted you are credible. If there is just one word that defines credibility and integrity it is consistency; consistency in your words, deeds and behaviors. One can define it as being *predicable*. For most people, there is a comfort zone with predictability.

There will be times, as an administrator, when you will be privy to confidential information. If asked to respond to a question about the topic, the proper step would be to simply state that you cannot discuss the matter at this time. Any attempt to side-step the question or to spin a response places your credibility and integrity in doubt. People can respect the need to not reveal certain information and they certainly can respect that response. However, they will believe you view them as idiots when they think you believe that they can be bought-off with a spin.

There is a subtle yet dominant underpinning that I need for you to see. There will be times when administrative decisions are made based upon things that, forgive me, everyone else cannot know. These are not covert, illegal issues but rather political (yes, I said it - but I will always be honest with you). The key is, as an administrator, how you present tough decisions, the details of which others may not be privy to and yet not seem as a dictator. Now you are talking LEADERSHIP!

Build strong relationships based upon integrity and credibility and that will lead to trust. Disagree but don't spin or exaggerate the truth. Have a "my way or the highway" attitude [**Grease Spot #8**] about relationships and you will eventually find yourself standing *by* the highway - *alone*.

The Art of Influencing

Leadership has been defined by Warren Bennis and Joan Goldsmith (1994), in their book Learning to Lead, as the art of influencing people to accomplish the mission of the organization. Principals cannot work in isolation. Isolation is a major grease spot [**Grease Spot #9**] on your high-wire. It is all about the relationships you seek out and the relationships you build. Who you influence and who influences you constitutes a series of progressive steps on the high-wire that, when taken with careful premeditation, can produce an effective school ethos.

In this regard, I once read a statement that made a great deal of sense. Actually, I have read many statements that have impacted me but this one stood out and I run it through my mind whenever I am about to get into a confrontational situation. The statement is, *manage your emotions while reading the emotions of others*. By maintaining your composure, you gain the advantage of not being seen as a knee-jerk reactor. This allows you to reflect on a situation and consider all of the tangential aspects associated with the situation. A principal listens to the voices of all stakeholders concerning their feelings and shows sympathy, understanding, and empathy. You must find ways to solve a problem and remain calm under emergent and changing conditions.

People respond to situations with varying degrees of emotion. You must notice how the person you are dealing with is physically and emotionally handling the issue and adapt your emotions and behaviors to best suit the situation. Certain situations call for stern discussions whereas other situations require a more open and caring conversation. The more adept you are at reading others' emotions the more successful you will be as an effective leader who builds positive personal relationships.

Fear is Good

Everyone, regardless of their position in life, is somewhat counter-balanced by the concept of fear. Fear keeps us on the straight and narrow and governs many of the things we do and most of the things we do not do. Many times the authority structure within an organization establishes what I call the *structural fear hierarchy*. Each of us has some structural fear because most of us have a boss of some kind – even if it is Freud's superego. There was a time when one of my superintendents was someone I had worked with for over twenty years and during that time I was a principal and he was an assistant principal in another building. As time passed and opportunities presented themselves, he self-selected to rise through the ranks and eventually became the superintendent of schools within the district. Someone who was my peer was now my boss.

Regardless of the extensive amount of time that I had known him throughout his rise to prominence within our district, there was a fear factor when I met with him *in his role* as superintendent. I was not afraid of him but that fear factor kicked in when I talk with him as his subordinate.

Be aware [**Grease Spot #10**] that you will have people looking at you, in your role as principal, as I looked at my superintendent. How you utilize this fear factor will be very interesting and indicative of you as a person *and* as a leader. I am not saying to abdicate your role or disparage the fact that whoever comes into your office or whoever you are talking with in the hallway will know that they are talking with their boss. You will be measured as a boss by the manner in which you utilize this fear factor. It will always be to your advantage to leverage the fear factor but be critically aware that the distance between utilizing this inbred, natural fear to your advantage and being seen as a bully is very, *very* close. The words *boss* and *bully* each start with the same letter – that is how close they are and it can be very easy for you to drift from one to the other.

Leaders/Mangers
Greasy if you Select One Over the Other [Grease Spot #11]

Leadership and management are not synonymous simply because they are two functions within a principal's organizational plan. There are many definitions of the word leadership. Warren Bennis' definition is one of the best. He defines leadership as "knowing yourself, having a vision that is well communicated, building trust among colleagues and taking effective action to realize your own leadership potential" (Bennis, Cummings and Spreitzer, 2001, p.45). When you compare Bennis' definition of leadership to the definition of management, which is "to control the movement or behavior of; to have charge of; direct; administer" (Agnes, 2004, p. 392), they are two different activities. The distinct difference between leaders and managers is that leaders deal with the people side of an organization providing inspiration, motivating people and creating opportunities. However, managers deal with the technical side managing day-to-day tasks such as supervising and controlling people by focusing them in the right direction. It is then blatantly clear that building principals are both leaders and managers. A too-heavy emphasis on one or the other, and things become unbalanced.

For example, school administrators are hired to perform managerial tasks such as directing, organizing, planning, and staffing. However, a person in an administration position such as principal of a school also needs to exhibit qualities of a leader such as motivation, empowering, and vision for the future in order to have a successful school. A lack of these leadership qualities can result in a less than effective school.

The Final Relationship – with Yourself

On a fairly regular and rotating basis, some people will support you, and others will *resist* you. As these people come into focus, be sure that in the process you don't end up creating *permanent* inside and outside groups based upon your relationship with them [**Grease Spot #12**]. Invite everyone to join you under the tent. Warren Bennis (2003) wrote that, "Leaders never lie to themselves, especially about themselves, they know their faults as well as their assets, and deal with them directly" (p. 32). Building relationships is the foundation of your effectiveness. Take care to include people or groups who agree and disagree with both you and each other. It is not about like or dislike, and it should never be about the establishment of power. It is all about your *use* of power! It is all about *how you lead!*

11

Chapter 2

Captain! Oh, Captain!

Imagine that you're the captain of a huge cruise ship about to set sail. The ropes that securely fasten your ship to the loading dock are let loose, and ever so slowly, your huge ocean liner moves away from the dock. You, as captain, are overseeing *all* that needs to be supervised; coordinating the freeing of the docking ropes, the entrance ramp being secured away, and seeing that everyone is in place and at their station. As your ship inches away from the dock it starts to get up to speed.

I have the same sensation each morning as I commence the school day. I guide the school through the opening rituals, making sure everything is in place as the first bells chime. However, the similarity between a ship's captain and the role of a building principal abruptly stops at this point. While a ship's captain can admirably run his or her ship from the bridge, the *last place* that a principal can effectively do their leadership *and* managerial operation is from their office [**Grease Spot #13**]. A building leader's presence *anywhere* but his or her office, during the school day, is a crucial factor in effectively managing and leading a school.

A significant managerial component is the people who work with you. James Kouzes & Barry Posner (2007) wrote in The Leadership Challenge, that you can't do it alone and that is the mantra of exemplary leaders. They go on and postulate that you simply cannot do extraordinary things alone. Collaboration is the master skill that enables teams to function effectively but it can be sustained only when you promote a sense of mutual reliance – the feeling that we're all in this together. From a managerial perspective, making sure that everyone not only knows their job functions but are also in a position to be able to do their job, creates a scenario where the whole is clearly the sum of its parts - and then some!

Just Five Minutes

One of the easiest steps to managing the operation of your school is to maintain a rote series of five minute meetings each morning, and the operative words here are - *each* and *morning*. As soon as my secretary arrives at school and becomes settled in, we touch base on what planned events are taking place during the day. Given that your day will be replete with a seemingly unending series of *unplanned events*, making sure that the scheduled ones have everything they need to be successful, can serve to help eliminate managerial blunders. We go over the day's calendar so that we are on the same page and so that she can field any inquiries, both internal and external, concerning any scheduled activity. The other critically important five-minute meeting is with your head custodian. The reality of needing a room specifically set up at a certain time of day, for a specific event, is a daily occurrence. Needing to utilize the same venue again, later in the day for a completely different reason and with a completely different set up, needs to be reaffirmed at the beginning of the day; not when students, teachers, and/or parents are standing at the threshold expecting the location to be ready.

I also spend a few minutes checking my calendar to see where I need to be during the day. What meetings are on my calendar and when I will be free to *wander* (seemingly aimlessly but never in reality is it aimless) *around* the school. Also, what special events are being conducted that I need to be at is also noted. Once plotted out, it then becomes my task to balance the events with phone calls, informal meetings, drop-bys, and the ever present, *do-you-have-a-minute* inquires?

And when you have informal meetings or a drop-by, *never sit down!* Conduct the meeting standing up. Have a *huddle* meeting. A huddle meeting is all business and no one nestles into a chair. Rude? No, they are effective and time saving. Trust me, try this *huddle* meeting approach at selected times when you need a fast touch-base kind of meeting.

Call me Elmer
The Principal as Managerial Glue

Management can be defined as directing people to accomplish a mission. I believe that leaders should focus on two fundamental elements: (a) the task of accomplishing the mission, and (b) supporting the people who accomplish the mission. Peter Northouse (2007) supported this premise in <u>Leadership: Theory and Practice</u>, a book based upon his research indicating that leadership is composed of two kinds of behaviors: task and relationship. Task behaviors facilitate goal accomplishment by helping stakeholders to achieve school-wide goals. Relationship behaviors help people to feel comfortable with themselves, with each other, and with the situation in which they find themselves - *and* with you! These are keys to highly effective management.

Managerial leadership is not based on your power and authority, but on principles, people skills, and your ability to encourage people. Leadership is "...a principle-based process of working together that produces trust, integrity, and breakthrough results by building true ownership and alignment in all aspects of the organization" according to E.W. Marshall. When a leader drives a school forward through a positive actions, changes will occur, and your managerial role will remain entwined with your relatively grease free high-wire.

The Thick of Thin Things

An old wives' tale (or maybe it is an old principals' tale), says not to get caught up in the unnecessary, especially when there are more importantly things to do. As an experienced principal, you will know what things will address themselves and the ones that will not. You will learn the difference between *urgent* and *important*. There are many times when a teacher will approach you with an issue and you will know that the issue does not need resolution at that moment. You will also know what needs immediate attention. Certainly a reasonable expectation, given the premise that you are not going to drop everything, all the time, to react to *every* issue brought to your attention. If this were the case, nothing would ever get done, just a great deal of issues being dropped.

You will be amazed at the number of these issues that will and can be handled extremely efficiently by the person coming to you with the issue. William James once said that the art of being wise is to know what to overlook. You've never said or indicated that you wanted them to handle the issue and yet many, many of these issues are just that – doable on their level. When you do eventually get to the issue and address the teacher again about it, many times you will hear, "Oh, I handled it myself." Of course, when to do this and when not to is a subtly that comes with time and experience.

John Maxwell (2003) contends that all tasks can be placed into one of the four following categories:

1) *High importance/High Urgency (Do it first).*
2) *High Importance/Low Urgency (Set deadlines and the work tasks into your daily routine).*
3) *Low Importance/High Priority (Find a quick way to complete these tasks or delegate).*
4) *Low Importance/ Low Urgency (Consider if these need to be done, if so delegate).*

It will be your task to utilize these four pigeonholes and utilize them as a *degreaser*. Your priority list needs to be set up in this fashion and as time goes by (I am talking years here not months) this will become automatic.

You will need to develop a sense of what is thick and what is thin. You will need to understand that what might initially appear as thin could get thick if you ignored it. You cannot learn this stuff from this book, or any other book and each school, of course, is different. Knowing your capabilities in reference to time on task and the strengths of your faculty and staff is tremendously helpful. Seen from the perspective of your faculty and staff, if everything was thick, you'd be running around like a chicken with its head cut off. Conversely, if you viewed everything as thin, you might be accused of being too laissez-faire, of not caring enough.

Just be aware that *everyone* who comes to you with an issue considers that issue to be thick [**Grease Spot #14**]!

Picture the Norm

One of my hobbies was photography, and many years ago when I was a classroom teacher, I wanted to take candid photos of my students working in class. For the first two weeks, I brought my camera into class but not loaded with film. (Yes film! Film was something loaded into a camera upon which a picture was produced.) I took shot after shot and pretended that the camera had film in it. After a period of time, the kids got used to me (and my camera) and instead of *mugging* for the camera, as they initially did, they got used to it, and I was able to get some great candid shots.

I use this analogy to illustrate that eventually your presence around the school will become the *norm* and not anything special, which is just what you want. One indicator of this is that there are times during the year when even my best intentions about being visible are not possible. Budget time, hiring time (interviews and demonstration lessons), student placement or scheduling for next year are four times that I am in classrooms less frequently (and that means I am there probably just once a week). I often get questioned by the teachers about where I have been due to the fact that they have not seen me walking around and even the students comment about not seeing me as often as they had grown accustomed. This is when you know that you are a visible presence.

Here is a great test of your visibility: If you walk into a classroom and the teacher stops to ask you, *"What is the matter?"* or *"Is there anything wrong?"* or *"Can I help you?"*, you haven't been around enough! In many ways, you become part of the classes because you are regularly there and join in activities when you are in the classroom. This *presence*, your visibility in and around school, should never be undervalued lest you create a huge grease spot [**Grease Spot #15**].

A former assistant principal and I used to have a funny little debate that took place each time we would be leaving the building to go to a meeting or to get a bite to eat (yes, you can go out of the building to eat). Our cars were parked adjacent to the student cafeteria. As we would leave the building and, if lunch was in session, it was her philosophy that she should leave the building via the student cafeteria. She felt that if the students saw her leaving, that they knew they had to be on their best behavior. I, on the other hand, would split off from her as we walked down the hallway and exited the building from a door that allowed me not to be seem by the kids. My theory was that if they still thought I was in the building, they would be better behaved. Silly? Yes. No. Maybe! You be the judge!

Knowing the Wire

Larry Frase and Robert Hetzel (1990) wrote the book, <u>Management by Wandering Around</u>. Nothing could be more accurate than the title and their premise. *Focused* and *purposeful* wandering around is the definitive way of ascertaining what is *really* happening in your school. There is no other way and no amount of dialogue with students, teachers and parents taking place in your office will allow you to get a handle on your school. I believe that two things happen when you are a visible presence, and I equate these occurrences to breathing - *breathing in* and *breathing out*. You need to do both and one is solely not effective for the desired purpose.

For purposes of this book, the concept of *breathing in* is the act of walking the halls and dropping into class after class. You are also in the cafeteria, the stairwells, the hallway during student arrival, on bus duty at the end of the day, and/or out in front of the school. You are watching. You are listening. You are observing. You are talking to, observing, and listening to adults and students alike. You are *breathing in* the ethos of your school, and by your mere presence, you are affirming that culture.

Are you making judgments? Of course you are! You are also seeing and sensing what *really* happens day-after-day. I attempt to pass through *every* classroom, every other day. It may be a short walk-through which can last only two-minutes, or at other times, I can hang-out a little longer depending on the circumstances within the classroom. This is, of course, is in addition to my formal observations of teaching that I perform. What is interesting is that, at times, the formal observation can be somewhat *plastic* as the teacher attempts to put his or her best foot forward during this *special*, forty-five minute time period. But, if you are in this teacher's classroom as often as you would be by wandering around, you will know if the observation is really a *scene* from

Cirque du Soleil just for your benefit. If you have been in the class often, you know what he or she really does daily not just when *company* has arrived, and things should feel the same.

You are like a sponge - you are absorbing! The most important thing I do is listen! What do you listen for, *what are you breathing in?* Certainly, one key dialogue that you will want to listen for is the manner, style, and tone in which classroom conversations take place. How do the teachers talk to kids? I want to hear strength, conviction, enthusiasm, *respect*, support, empathy, humor, excitement, and guidance. I want teachers to convey a sense that they are facilitating an exploration or journey and that he/she is on this journey *with* the students. This may be the sixteenth time (year) that the teacher is teaching this particular lesson but it had better sound as though they are as excited about it as they were the first time they taught it. It may be a cliché, but the best teachers do not enjoin their students to learn. They join them in learning!

I also listen for how students react and response to teachers. Is there a respect for him or her as an adult who has something to offer? Effective teachers are seen by students as someone with something to offer. Effective teaching is part relationship between class members (students) and teacher and the interaction between the two. Students have to feel that this person respects them for who they are and that they are comfortable in the manner and way they are being perceived by him or her and how they are being taught. This is certainly an important component as students get older and move up through the system, but this can also be seen even in the primary grades.

Single direction teacher-to-student only monologue is not teaching, but rather it is lecturing *to* students. There is no engagement, no ownership on the part of the students (and probably the teacher for that matter). When teachers think that students are the storage containers into which they are trying to pour information, that is not teaching, and certainly not quality education. Real teaching is the sound of interaction between students and teacher and the facilitation of student-to-student dialogue. By being in classrooms on a regular basis, and by wandering around the school, you get little threads each and every day that ultimately form your understanding of the tapestry of your school. Please do not confuse my wandering around with the 3-minute walk-throughs of recent fame. Nothing will distract a teacher more than you walking through their class with a clipboard and a pen – as per the official 3-minute walkthrough process. That process interrupts and intimidates and is probably counterproductive.

The second part of the breathing concept - *breathing out* - I equate to your ability to make leadership and managerial decisions based upon what you have taken (breathed) in. This encompasses your knowledge-base of your school, its students, staff, teachers and parents. *Your* presence and visibility goes a long way to establishing the ethos of the school. Never underestimate the power of your title, *Principal*, your role as leader and manager, the importance of your vision as a leader and the effectiveness of your presence. Sans your ability and willingness to *breathe in*, you will never effectively *breathe out!*

No Open Door Policy

I do not have an *open door* policy. To me, an open door policy infers that I am in my office - waiting for someone or for some issue to be brought to my attention (we will discuss *Ostrich Administration* later). I would, respectfully, suggest *not* having an open door policy but rather have an *open hallway* policy, an *open cafeteria* policy, and an *open bus duty* policy. The best managerial endeavor is visibility and establishing a presence. Warren Bennis (2001) attributed the success of a leader to his or her ability to not only relate to people, but also to *engage* people so that they are motivated. You best engage people by going to them and allowing them to have access to you; not in your realm (your office) but rather in their venue.

Your Desk: It Will Never Be Big Enough to Hide Behind

There are principals who tend to *center themselves* in their office [**Grease Spot #16**]. They think that their school can be steered from the helm. While this works well for cruise ships, it is the antithesis of effective school leadership. The office is the last place that you will be able to lead from effectively. In essence, you are hiding behind the name (principal) on the door and the desk in the room. The true basis of leadership and a true leader does not stand behind their title or sit behind a desk, but rather stands in front of their title and out away from their desk. These people view leadership as a *function and process* rather than seeing it as a role or position.

As you engage in the discipline of management by being visible, others will be more inclined to work with you. People must see and will, subsequently, respect that you are physically and fully engaged in the managerial process. You cannot, in my opinion, be successful if you direct from your office. People must see and *feel* that you are fully engaged in the leadership process by being fully engaged and visible in the building.

The Faculty and Grease

Years ago, my head custodian came to me and said he had made a sign Reserved for the Principal and wanted to post the sign on the wall in front of a parking space. I asked him where the space was and he replied, "the one closest to the door of the school." Without being condescending, I asked him, *"Why that spot?"* He gave me the typical, you are the principal response and, therefore, your parking spot should be closest to the door. *Why?*

I think asking the question, *why*, is the mindset that I would suggest *you* have in terms of your relationship with the staff members of the school. *Why* should your spot be any different or preferential? Should you be the one who gets less wet on a rainy day? *Why?* Should you be the one not trudging through knee high snow? *Why?* I would suggest to you that one of the first things you should do when you become principal of a school and a sign like the one the custodian wanted to put up for me exists, ask the custodian to take it down. *Why?* You tell me!

The high-wire may be fully engulfed in grease [**Grease Spot #17**] and somewhat permanently, based upon your relationship with your faculty. You will inevitably be judged too quickly by them collectively, but your strength and strongest potential is your *individual* work with and support of them. Just remember that kids, parents, and even central office people come and go, but your most consistent stakeholders will *always be* your faculty.

Faculties, as a group, want fairness, consistency, and a willingness to be heard with dependable feedback regularly given to them. Take all requests seriously and respectfully, and follow through with, at the very least, a good reason why something cannot happen. Saying we do not have the money available to cover your request is an understandable and realistic response, but I submit, not a *complete* response. Nor is indicating the superintendent or board of education did not like the idea and/or would not support it.

While all of the above may, in fact, be true, it is psychologically defeating to hear it. If you are supportive of the initiative and for the reasons stated above the initiative is not supported at a higher level, rather than just indicating the above, a better course of action would be to be simpatico, an approach of we are in this together. Indicate that it was a great idea and what can we do *together* to get this on track for possible implementation down the road. I can think of dozens of initiatives that were initially proposed and took years to get approved. Money, philosophy, how the needs were presented all had a part in this process.

My suggestion is never give up on a *great idea* that will assist kids directly and/or assist teachers who are assisting kids. Plan together with faculty members who presented the initiative. Ask the people who denied acceptance, why it was denied and what would be a next step to getting something like this approved? Here is the most important key word that, when utilized properly, can move mountains. Indicate to your superintendent you want to *pilot* something! A *pilot project!* I have seen this word *pilot* move mountains, and I swear you could probably get funding to try and float the Rock of Gibraltar - if you couch the effort as a pilot program.

Also, think of the positive impact this will have on you and the members of your faculty who are pushing for the initiative. You guys are working together against all odds to plan for the sale of your initiative to the superintendent and board of education, followed by *implementation*, assessment and analysis of the results. All of this in a collaborative effort between you and your staff. You have bonded in a unified cause! You could not buy that relationship with 100 years of the donuts and coffee you bring to faculty meetings.

One of my underlying, foundational, and most prevalent philosophies is that my job (that of a principal) is to hire the very best people; provided these professionals with the atmosphere and tools in which they can thrive and then get out of their way and let them teach. I truly believe I am their servant and I exist to provide for them, so that they can do their job with as little interference as I can arrange for in the school. Don't ever verbalize this to them, *just do it!*

The Faculty Room

A principal's relationship with the faculty and staff has always been one of the more fascinating aspects of orchestrating a school as well as creating a grease-free path on your high-wire. What principal has not had the experience of approaching the school's faculty room and heard talking and laughter, turned the doorknob, opened the door, and walked into the room. At that instant, all of the conversation and laughter suddenly stops and people scramble to shift to a new topic. This, in and of itself, doesn't indicate your high-wire is greased. This is a natural *us* –v- *them*, *worker* –v- *management* kind of thing.

Take heart, *they were* talking about you either in a good way or a not-so-good way. In my opinion, the faculty room is just that; a room for the *faculty* and it is not your room or place. I believe you have placed a spot of grease on your high-wire [**Grease Spot #18**] if you attempt to invade a territory that is not yours. I believe it is not your territory and that you should respect the faculty's right and, more importantly, their *need* to have a place to go and talk - *about anything*. If you are going to be a principal like me who is all over the place (some would suggest like *fertilizer*, which has both good and not so good connotations), then a place for the faculty is important. I avoid the room like the plague, and besides, what could they possibly be saying about me anyway?

Well, it probably has something to do with my last memo or email or comments made at a faculty meeting or the *have-you-heard-about* kind of rumor. Sometimes the door closes behind someone, who sits down at the table and, in front of everyone, says something like, *"You won't believe what that ____ of a ____ did to me"* (by the way, they are probably referring to you)! There was something that was seen as unfair that was perpetrated on them. These people are seeking solace and a comfort zone in a setting where they think one exists.

Wonder Bread with Extra Mayo

When I was a teacher attempting to enjoy my lunch in the faculty room, inevitably one of my colleagues would be sitting there or enter the room complaining about a certain administrator and what he or she, *did to them!* At times, there would even be words of support and/or encouragement from others for this teacher. As I munched on my Bologna on Wonder Bread with extra mayo, I was glad to have something in my mouth that prevented me from saying what I was really thinking. This particular teacher was a terrible teacher. She was always the last one in school each day and she beat the buses out of the parking lot at the end of the day. She was always complaining about how unfair *they* were to her and sought to undermine the administration at every opportunity and, at the same time, gain support for her self-perceived, woeful situation caused by "those administrators."

My thought was that finally there was an administrator who would not accept her unprofessional manner and her poor teaching skills/practices. I am also convinced that I was not the only person in the room who felt the same way, yet no one would challenge her. So she had her soapbox. She had her place to vent. She had her place to find a captive audience willing (or not) to hear what she had to say. I am not so sure that good administrators really have to be concerned about what is happening in faculty rooms. Why sweat the things you cannot control? All things being equal, I have always been astonished at the ethos of the faculty room. Grown adults with professional degrees, capable of intelligent discourse on a variety of subjects will sit with muted attention while some sub-par slacker attempts to rally people to his or her line of action or thinking.

I am convinced that teachers want administrators to do their job. I am convinced that when colleagues like that use *rancor*, there are many who are silently applauding that they have been stood up to and exposed. I am convinced that your *stock rises significantly* in the minds of *quality* educators when they can sit back and say to themselves, *finally someone has the guts enough to put this person in their place and not be intimidated by him or her.* Teachers want outstanding colleagues working next to them and that is your responsibility. Do you know whose fault it is when poor teachers exist in a school system? An administrators fault!

As a neophyte principal, the silence of the faculty room upon my entrance was deafening. I recall a remedial reading teacher who loudly protested my evaluation of her poor pedagogy. She sat in the faculty room and indicated to everyone within earshot and who had the capability of hearing and understanding the spoken word, that I had no knowledge of her process and her methodology. How dare I write an unflattering evaluation of her work! However, she never shared the evaluation with the faculty, rather only *her overview* of my questioning and finding fault with her methodology.

I, of course, could not address *any* component of the issue in a sort of point-counter-point setting because it would be unprofessional of me to discuss someone else's evaluation sans their permission and she was not about to let the entire picture out - just the part she wanted known.

So this teacher was telling everyone that I was forcing her to change a process that she had been utilizing for over fifteen years. *"How dare him!!!!!!!!!!!!!!!!!"* That is what the faculty heard and, in point of fact, I was *not asking* her to change - actually, I was *demanding* it!

Punch and Judy

What the faculty didn't hear was *why* I wanted the change. This remedial reading teacher met with small groups of between five to seven students, three times per week for thirty minutes per session. Her charge was to increase decoding skills as well as comprehension skills for these children who were all performing well below grade level. Her methodology was to have the students write and, subsequently, read a short play with an accompanying puppet show. The kids would come up with various story lines and then write parts for themselves and each other. Hey! Not a bad methodology! Kids involved in writing and reading their own work - works for me, so far. On two of the days (out of three per week) she would have the kids writing and editing their work. On the third day of *every* week, she would have the kids *make their puppets*. Let me repeat this just so that you do not miss it or so that you can take copious notes on this trend setting, pedagogical intervention strategy to increase decoding skills and reading comprehension; *these kids made puppets!* So, *one third of the time* that the students should be getting remedial assistance in reading and comprehension they were, in essence, in remedial *art* class.

I suggested to the teacher that the students make the puppets at home. I suggested to the teacher that maybe they could make the puppets as part of their regular art class. I suggested to her to talk with the art teacher. I even volunteered to do that for her. I suggested to the teacher that they could make the puppets during recess, when we couldn't go outdoors due to inclement weather. I made many suggestions over a two-year period. I even sat with her once and approached it from the perspective of how she was such an outstanding reading teacher and that her students were missing a third of their time with her based upon the fact that they were not in direct contact with her working on reading. Nothing worked with her. She liked the down time that puppet making gave her.

Can it Get Worse?

It gets worse! After all the writing and puppet making (and those puppets took weeks to make) the students would *perform* their puppet show. After all their effort to write and edit the script, I supported this component. So they performed once for their parents, a few times for all of the teacher's other remedial sections (and, factor in, this teacher's other sections did the same thing and performed also), and this went on and on and on. Weeks of the same performance, over and over again!

Where was their remediation? Where was the content of reading strategies that would assist students as the reading requirements became increasingly more complex as they moved up through the grade levels? I clocked the amount of non-instructional time and it was unbelievable. However, all this teacher ever told anyone in the faculty room (and elsewhere) was how dare this new principal *"tell me how to teach"*, and I had to remain mute on the subject. When push came to shove, and I was unable to convince her of anything, my evaluation directed her to alter (I never utilized the word, *stop*) what she was doing and spend time with the students using more traditional methods and in a more traditional remedial setting on *each* of the three days she was with them. I did not want the puppets made during remedial reading and I limited the number of performances to four. I had no problem with the puppet plays as components of her methodology but rather with the time it consumed. The only thing that ever made it into the faulty room was, of course, *"look what he is doing to my program!"* But there were people in that room that were glad (I learned years later) that *finally, someone had stood up to her.* They knew she had spent much of her class time in arts and crafts instead of reading instruction, and they resented it.

So the faculty room is filled with teachers pretending loyalty to a poor performing colleague and yet thinking, *good, finally someone has this clown's number and is doing something about him or her.* You have added significantly to your credibility and gained respect. You are well on your way to asking for quality instruction and professional demeanor and have put your actions where your mouth is. People will look at you differently. It wasn't until years later, after that teacher retired, that one of her fellow reading teachers confided in me that for years people knew what she was doing, did not agree with her pedagogy, but no one had the guts to stand up to her until me, and my stock (and sand on my beach) had risen significantly because of my position. G-d, I wish I knew that back then!

Effective Faculty (Grade Level and/or Departmental) Meetings Leads to Less Grease

If the truth be told, most people do not like and do not respond well to faculty meetings. Unless you can guarantee a meeting will end with everyone walking away with new and/or useful information (which should be the only reason to have a faculty meeting in the first place) your time spent together will seem worthless and most people will not be happy [**Grease Spot #19**]. Keep in mind that you are asking people to come in early before school or stay after school, which potentially presents a mess of grease to begin with!

One solution is to have an agenda and send it out prior to the meeting and stick to it! This will serve to define the purpose of your meeting and will effectively respond to the question of *why are we here?* Holding to time ranges are important. Meetings ending early are one thing but meetings that drag out because you did not stick to the agenda or got sidetracked or allowed members in the meeting to move off of the agenda is not good.

It is critically important to start your faculty meetings on time. A 3:00 pm meeting is a 3:00 pm meeting! It does not start at 3:08 or 3:14. You need to show respect for everyone who was present and ready to go at 2:58 pm! If you indicate the faculty meeting will start at 3:00 and you consistently start the meeting at 3:10, when do you think faculty will eventually arrive at your 3:00 pm meeting – you got it – 3:10! And never, *never*, <u>ever</u> repeat what you started to talk about (in other words, start the meeting over again) for those arriving late – <u>never</u>. Nothing upsets those arriving on time more than getting the same information repeated because of late arrivers. Whoever gets there late is still accountable for what was discussed. They can ask a colleague later what they missed. What message do you give when you hold a meeting and provide no ending time, just an open block with no time limits. The message is talk all you want and take all the time you need. Not the message anyone wants to hear at the end of a long day of teaching! You might as well walk into the room with a sleeping bag and a Coleman stove! *People work smarter when parameters of the meeting include a time frame.*

Faculty meetings must be seen as having a purpose beyond that which can be accomplished via a memo, email, or personal discussions. Therefore, the importance of an agenda so that faculty members can be prepared for the issue(s) on the table is important. During the meeting, you need to be in as much control as possible and yet allow for unfettered discussion, pro and con, directed at the issue(s) and towards a mutually agreed upon fruition. The potential grease here is balancing running an effective and efficient meeting (with an eye toward the clock) that, at the same time, allows for open discussion.

There are several techniques that can help to generate ideas and commence a focus on an issue. One is to have a period of time where everyone makes suggestions, which are written down in clear view without any criticism. People can then explain their idea *for a minute or two*, and after that, each idea is evaluated by the group, one by one. This brainstorming technique can be very effective.

Success depends on the cooperation of the people at the meeting, and it is often a good idea to let the group decide what ideas they will utilize. Remember, if you head down this road of an open sharing of ideas and possible solutions, you are equally as committed to the results as generated by the faculty. Therefore, be cautious and judicious with the concepts and issues that you send to the faculty!

If people have a hand in decisions, they have a stake in seeing them work. Involving people in decision-making can lower their anxiety and raise the quality of their work. But the involvement must be real. Unless the faculty can help to define the problem and potential solutions – and is allowed to select which path to take – they may distrust you because you were only giving lip service in asking for their input. Remember: *distrust = grease!*

Sometimes, an issue is too extensive and/or complicated to be resolved in an hour to an hour-and-a-half faculty meeting. You have, however, made the issue/concept clear to everyone and have even started the thought process rolling. It might be prudent, at that time, to set up an advisory committee made up of faculty in the room to meet and eventually report back at the next faculty meeting about the issue. Setting up a committee to deal with specific problems, and letting those committee members recommend solutions, may be a fast and effective way to work. This power and involvement will also make the faculty's job more rewarding.

Healthy Conflict

Some conflict is good if arguments do not get personal and people are not driven to intransigence. Personal criticism should never be allowed, and your role is to enable critical discourse that moves toward resolution but does not breakdown communication. Be aware, though, *too little* criticism or commentary, may suggest a pervasive feeling that nothing real will come from the meeting and people just want it to end. The best meetings have some criticism, but it is aimed at ideas, not people, and is grounded in problems with the ideas.

Action Steps

Ask someone to write up what I call *action steps* near the end of each meeting. Action steps include a summary of what was decided, *what each person or group of people has agreed to do* (this solidifies commitments and serves as a written reminder), and specific deadlines. Conclude with the day, time, and purpose of the next meeting. At the next meeting, the first order of business should be the status of the action steps.

Meetings have gotten a bad rap because many meetings are unproductive and dull. But they have both a place and a high potential in schools looking to be proactive, or find solutions to ongoing school-wide issues. Great meetings can increase how people see you as a leader and as a manager, so be cognizant of your time *and their time!*

1. Have a realistic agenda.

2. Encourage feedback.

3. Ideas, activities, and commitment to the organization improve when members see their impact on the decision-making process.

4. Keep conversation focused on the topic.

5. Feel free to ask for only constructive and non-repetitive comments.

6. Tactfully end discussions when they are getting personal, becoming destructive, unproductive or repetitive.

7. Write up and distribute minutes within two days.

Chapter 3

The Process of Change
The only person who likes change is a baby with a wet diaper! -
Mark Twain

We all have to negotiate change every day of our lives, but a dynamic environment like a school multiplies the effect tenfold. You will be addressing change from the moment you walk into your first building as principal. In point of fact, your mere presence as the new principal is a huge change everyone will need to get comfortable with. I would suggest to you that it will be the *pace* of that change, the *degree* of change and, most importantly, the *effectiveness* of that change that will serve as the basis of your reputation and, subsequently, your effectiveness. These will also serve as a regulator of the amount of change-grease on your high-wire [**Grease Spot #20**]. Become, in the coming years, a *student of change*. Attempt to gain a working knowledge of how to encourage it, how to regulate it, and how to gain the trust of others so that you can effectively and seamlessly apply it. Never attempt change just to make a change to put *your stamp* on the place but never avoid it when necessary.

Change is complex and sometimes painful to orchestra, but it is inevitable in every organization and is rarely an option. Robins and Judge in their book Organizational Behavior (2009) reminds us that no organization maintains a "stable environment" and even those once predictably stable industries are witnessing "turbulent change" (p. 619). Since change is inevitable and complex, it must be managed and led with knowledge and grace in order for the change to be successful. With change comes the inevitable stress and magnitude of dealing with the planned or unplanned change. So, it isn't simply how you conduct the change but how you manage the potential *resistance* to change and the potential *stress* on the participants. Michael Fullan (1999) notes in his book Change Forces that change is mandatory, growth is optional.

Probably nothing will be more important in a school-wide sense, than how you deal with the process of change. It can be one long grease spot on your high-wire. How you bring about lasting and effective change will be a measurement of your success. Change mechanisms need to be consistent and open. The age of benevolent dictatorships where the principal was the sole and exclusive decision-maker no longer exists. First of all, you do not want all that responsibility. You may have it but why not bring additional intellect into the decision-making process.

You will need to effectively build consensus among stakeholders by keeping them involved, well informed, interested, and with the understanding that you feel their opinions are important. At just about every inch on your high-wire, you will be negotiating change, building a consensus for change, brainstorming change concepts, directions, and finally implementing and, subsequently, evaluating change. You cannot avoid making changes because a school that is standing still is a school slipping backwards.

How do you build consensus with teachers, parents, members of parent-teacher organizations, student groups and with fellow administrators within your district? Can you manipulate the process or at the very least, use the process in such a manner that you get what you want? I know, I know, consensus means taking the idea from a broad spectrum of shareholders and building a direction that *everyone* can *buy* into. The problem with these high ideals is that at the end of the day, you, the principal, are still going to be evaluated on the end the result. I don't know about you, but if I am going to be held accountable for the result of anything, I want to be in charge or, at least, have a tremendous amount to say about the concept, the goal, *and* the process.

Think how silly you are going to sound when something does not come to fruition that was originally planned for and you, the building principal, say it was the committee's idea. A leader *always* takes all the blame when things go wrong and, conversely, always shares the kudos when things go well. The principal's power is the antithesis of leadership by committee and yet there needs to be a seat under the tent for all stakeholders.

The Consensus Gate

Reaching consensus doesn't mean everyone agrees with the change and how to achieve it, but it does mean that no one opposed it so intensely that it was discarded. I believe the first gate of this process is to determine what gets to go through the consensus process. What can you, as a principal, allow to be a shared decision-making team issue? The better job that you can do at filtering (cover word for *controlling*) what goes to the decision-making team allows you to be in control of the issues in your building. I don't think I can prescribe what these issues would be. I believe that for each principal and, subsequently, for each school that would be different.

One of the guidelines that I utilize is the, *how many people is it going to take to introduce and monitor this process successfully?* If we are talking about better control and behavior patterns in the lunchroom, I am not going to be able to pull that off by myself. Every teacher on duty in the cafeteria needs to take a degree of responsibility and, more importantly, *ownership* in the process and an interest in the outcome. The same thing must be applied to student behavior in the hallways. It cannot just be the building principal but rather everyone needs to be a part of the process.

On the other hand, if it is something that I can monitor on my own; for instance, professional development opportunities, then I am not sure that this is an issue for a decision-making team. As you filter in the issues and concepts you can better control the potential outcome. At some point, you would want to feel that the faculty would look to you no matter what the issue and seek your approval and support of their consensus. You will really have something special going if your faculty acquiesces to you and your leadership and is respectful of what you do and do not send to the shared decision-making committee.

If everyone is empowered then change can be far less painful for everyone – including you. I also think that sometimes people in school districts have knee-jerk reactions to issues. That is harmful because then there doesn't appear to be a plan (either short term or long term). In my opinion, that is why making change a part of the process (or more accurately, the process for potential change) is critically important.

Back to that Trust and Credibility Thing (again)

The opportunity for change will come after you build interpersonal support and trust – the timing is important because grease is always waiting [**Grease Spot #21**]. The capacity for change is inherently based upon the capital that you, as a principal, have established based upon that trust. Assessing the culture for change of an organization takes an administrator about one year. Only by sharing a few cycles of communication, listening to feedback, and observing reactions to real situations can an administrator really know and understand the people with a dedicated interest in the school. So, I reiterate, earn *trust* first!

There will be cliques to discover, interpersonal relationships to understand, a history to learn (the school's culture of change), politics, dependencies, strengths and weaknesses. Only after about a year will a principal know who the early supporters are, who the recalcitrants are, who will resist change, who will support change, and why. It is only after this year that the principal can begin to *anticipate* reactions and plan for them, rally support groups, establish trust with likeminded stakeholders, and really start the process of rolling out new plans and procedures.

I think it might be *unreasonable* to assume you can progress without ever alienating anybody or any group. Sometimes, just for cooperating or performing in harmony with one group, you alienate a group that is philosophically opposed to that group's idea(s). By taking a stance, you inevitably alienate extremes from that stance. The high-wire balancing act is, at times, subtle and the smallest of missteps or miss-reads can lead to peril.

Challenges and Resistance to Change

When the security and comfort of a person's environment is challenged or changed, fear and discomfort become present and can result in resistance. Some employees even feel threatened, or personally targeted, and start building emotional barriers in resistance to the change. If you have a good understanding of the change and ideas related to the change process, you just might be able to plan around resistance. People often hold on tight to what feels comfortable, and sometimes principals underestimate what it will take to get individuals *out of their comfort zone* and *into a newer zone*. Don't underestimate what it might take to make some people consider something new. Comfort zones are – well – comfortable! To understand how to deal with change, you must understand potential resistance.

While leaders do set the direction for change they also need to have tolerance for and understanding of those who resist so they can help them move forward. There will always be resisters and if you do not understand about the process that stakeholders must go through in order to embrace the changes that need to be made to move the school forward, then the change may never happen. The resisters can influence others both in and out of the faculty room (you remember the faculty room) in a negative way and a leader needs to be ahead of them in knowing the stages of the change process as well as who his/her supporters are. The principal must be the leader who inspires and motivates his/her staff. Everyone emotionally is in a different place as far as embracing change and you need to know each staff member and respond to the level of need/concern of each member and help each move forward. *Always* remember that all change is emotionally charged – even change you know is positive and many people seem to support.

You need to be aware of why the energy behind new initiatives often diminishes over time, even when teachers and staff members share a commitment to an initiative. There can be many reasons as to why commitment diminishes over time. For one thing, generally there is a great deal of energy at the beginning of any undertaking. There is a sense that change is coming and that change will be for the better. However, as time goes on, that energy can diminish. Results often do not come as soon as expected and roadblocks are rarely discussed in the opening phases of any project. When these roadblocks and other problems present themselves, energy and commitment tends to be drained. At such times, you can find yourself pushing a boulder up hill.

New initiatives also come with promises and expectations. These promises and expectations give all members a sense of hope and excitement. As the process moves forward, the focus is rarely on the expectations, but seems to turn toward issues and problems. I also believe that your strength and determination of leadership can also diminish over time. Principals, like everyone else, tend to lose energy and momentum along the way. It can be because things are not working out smoothly *or* because there are just too many bumps in the road and you become discouraged. It can also be that your attention (and time and energy) must be diverted to other issues. It can be very difficult to keep yourself and others focused and upbeat throughout the entire change process; however, taking your eyes off the target would be a *serious* [**Grease Spot #22**] miscalculation.

The last concept you will need to understand and embrace is that change really takes a long time to be effective. Too often, we expect change to come swiftly, and that is just not the case. Members involved in the process must be in for the long haul, and accept that effective, long-lasting change can take quite a long period of time. Machiavelli wrote, "There is nothing more difficult to carry out, nor more doubtful of success, nor more dangerous to handle, than to initiate a new order of things."

The Shamu Factor

In the context of building relationships and collaborative decision-making, you will need to know with whom to share information, ideas, and initiatives. You will need to know who to bring into the collaborative process when you see where the Splash Zone will be. Visitors to Sea World are informed that if they sit in certain rows at the Shamu Whale Show, they are going to get wet! These rows are called the Splash Zone. Utilize the same concept when decisions need to be made and people will be, subsequently, impacted (splashed upon). Ask yourself, *who is sitting in the Splash Zone?*

People with an interest in decisions affecting the school are in the Splash Zone and the makeup of that group usually varies from one issue to the next. Their interconnections reach not only from you to them but, by *your example*, are created among them as well. It is how you work with and treat these relationships that will establish the culture by which these groups will communicate with each other *and with you*. Leadership that demonstrates support for each relationship seeks to maintain interdependence and cooperation between all groups for the good of the students in your school. These relationships within the context of your school constitutes the ethos of your school and demonstrates your consideration and awareness of the status and stature of each stakeholder group.

Effective Professional Development

According to Gordon (2004), professional development that focuses on one-time workshops or programs with little teacher relevance can be viewed as inconsequential by most teachers. Although many of the programs may be interesting, without application opportunities the information is not used and, therefore, is lost. Teachers have very busy schedules outside of the classroom and they spend a lot of time planning lessons, correcting papers, and gathering materials. Professional development that does not assist with these tasks becomes a burden rather than helpful.

As we explore improvement of instruction and the best efforts of principals to improve instruction, the notion of a school *as a community of learners* constantly echoes in my mind. I am always filled with questions and self-doubt about how best to achieve that *community* concept even as a reasonably accomplished principal with a nationally recognized, award - winning school.

One of the key components of creating a grease-free high-wire is to have a staff that is always moving forward in terms of skill-set development and professional growth. A faculty that is standing still in terms of professional growth is a faculty sliding backwards to a comfortable spot with no challenges. As strange as it sounds, it can be very easy to forget about professional development unless there is a mantra of life-long learning consistently reverberating in your head [**Grease Spot #23**].

The bottom line is that many times useless professional development (PD) is the annual or semi-annual Staff Development or Superintendent's Conference Day professional development with paid motivational speakers who get people fired up – for a while. One-time shots in the arm usually translate to very little long term. Your staff development day focus must be refocused again and again within your school at intervals that support the initiative and that works toward bringing the initiative to a successful fruition. There also needs to be a great deal of proactive discussion on the PD focus prior to the larger Staff Development Day opportunities. Most times professional development is seen by central office administration as a district-wide event. I know that there could be wonderful opportunities for *building-wide* PD, if only central office administration would allow schools (principals and faculty) to act individually. I liken this to only one laboratory in the United States being allowed to search for a cure for cancer. A *this must be done here and only here* mindset creates little room for dynamic enhancement and serves one-size fits all mediocrity! Think of the possibilities if the faculty and building level administration in each building were allowed to explore pedagogical and curricula advancement rather than everyone in a district having to march along to the tune of the same topic each year at Staff Development Day.

The question I always ask is, *"When is the best time for Professional Development?"* If the only PD that takes place consists of those special staff development days, then that can equate to next to nothing. It might, in fact, equate to less than nothing as teachers might resent the time spent hearing about something that they know will not be followed up on or might have negligible impact on their school and the needs of the school's teachers and students. So, please pick a time (A through E) you like for professional development.

- A) <u>After School</u>? PD should be taking place when people are at their best and I am not convinced that after school is that time. I don't know about you, but after seven-plus hours of working with kids, the last thing my mind is ready for is two hours of PD.

- B) <u>Before School</u>? I, at least, have to add it to the list just so the list is complete. However, got an extra hour or two before the day starts? I am not going to wait for the answer, so just move on to C.

- C) <u>During vacation periods</u>? Christmas/Hanukah, Easter/Passover, Presidents' Day/Week. Again, I will respectfully move on.

- D) <u>Saturdays</u>?

- E) <u>During summer vacation</u>? Yes, professional development can and does take place during the week after school closes or a few days before school opens but - for selected personal. It is not widespread or universal, in most cases.

I think I have run out of possibilities! Wait! I have not!

Potentially Effective PD Time

I believe the most effective time for professional development is smack in the middle of the school day. Think about it, please. You have everything you need: equipment, materials, people, venue, and the kids. Planning professional development opportunities during the school day works for everyone! You must be willing to invest the time and the duration of time (years) that this slow moving tortoise of a PD initiative entails, but I am telling you that slow and steady *wins* the race.

The trick is can you schedule and/or arrange for teachers in the same department and/or teaching the same courses and/or working on the same grade level to be together? Certainly, common preparation times are the most logical and the first place to look. With the common prep-times comes the ability to place on the docket joint endeavors to enrich the teachers. Visits to other classrooms to work with teachers are do-able. Imagine having three teachers in a room at one time working on pedagogy *with* the kids! In schools that have permanent substitute teachers, and there are days when the substitutes are not assigned, that can allow for a classroom teacher to be freed up to co-teach and/or observe another teacher.

Also, never negate *your role*, as principal, in the professional development process. In addition to the scheduling component, you and your assistant(s) (if you have them) can cover classes so that teachers can work together for a period or two. Think of the message that is sent to your teachers. You are willing to give up part of your day to cover classes so teachers have an opportunity to grow. That is a *significant* message from a principal to the staff about how you view the importance of professional development. Schedule these opportunities as you would schedule an observation. Talk with staff about who they want to work with, what will be accomplished, what follow up will be necessary, and when that would take place.

I am not saying that after or before school is totally out of the picture (think faculty meetings). I am just suggesting that those before and after school PD opportunities will be better accepted by the teachers knowing that these meetings are *part of* a system, not *the only part* of a system.

Having a structure in place to foster PD is just one piece of this two-piece puzzle. The development of a universal understanding by stakeholders of *where* PD should be focused is the second piece. There should be a system to determine where yearly PD efforts need to go - a long range plan. And, if presented effectively to your superintendent, you might be able to fly on your own for a little ways as a school instead of those district-wide meetings. Nothing feels better than that.

Probably the underlining and foundational component of any academic needs assessment that is foundational to effective professional development would be data from assessment of student progress via test results and alternative means of assessing student progress. As a basis for professional development, teachers *must* gather to discuss responses to the following:

What do we want kids to learn in each grade level and from grade to grade?

What do we want kids to know when they leave our school?

What do we want kids to be able to do well?

Where Are You Going?

I am sure you have heard the following truism countless times, *if you don't know where you are going, how will you know when you get there?* Developing a plan, a long-range plan, three years out, is a great start and foundation. Where do we want to be in three years, and what are the benchmarks we want to achieve at the end of each year on the journey? Absent the game plan, haphazard events can take place that are not even tangential to the plan but are enough to sidetrack or cause people to lose focus. Issues of concern need to be discussed and up-dates as to rates of progress noted. Specific components may need to be readdressed but do not represent a failure but rather a re-assessment and redeployment of focus with an eye still firmly fix on the desired fruition.

Celebrate accomplishments and revisit (repair) less than effective results. Do so in a purposeful manner and with the confidence to take a step or two back when needed. One way to ensure annual progress is establishing a laser beam, school-wide focus that all stakeholders buy into. Selecting one priority as the focus for all or most of the professional development offered during the year may seem small but firm baby steps are better than large uncontrolled attempts at leaping. Shared control and decision-making broaden the basis of a support system and lead to shared responsibility and accountability.

Use faculty meetings as opportunities for group interactions centering on the PD initiative. Inform the faculty of the next phase of the PD and what has been accomplished to date. Provide time for small groups to meet during the faculty meeting to plan for upcoming components. This is a good time to center on global aspects of the PD for the year and to refocus, if necessary.

Professional development can only be effective if something positive happens as a result. This is why the one-day, guru flying into the district, dis-pensing their wares as if they were snake-oil salesmen from the back of a covered wagon in the 1800s never works. Without follow-up activities, very, very few participants use new skills.

How Are You Viewed?

I have previously written about your involvement in the process as a principal willing to give up his or her time to support staff collaboration. What is also critically important is for you to observe in classrooms, ask teachers about their progress, and develop assessment standards and instruments to measure the impact of new instructional techniques on student achievement. This is where the process can get a little greasy in terms of your professional development portion of your high-wire.

Your ability to be out there, to watch, listen, participate in the professional development initiative(s) and not be seen as someone who is conducting an observation or evaluation of the teacher's effectiveness will be a test of your relationship with your staff. Are you seen as a helper or as an overseer? Are you seen as someone taking in information to move the initiative forward or are you being seen as someone looking to see who is not effective. The difference is *huge,* and how your presence is perceived will make all the difference.

Whenever any new program enters our school, I never *formally* evaluate/observe a teacher working within that initiative. Do I come in and watch? *Yes.* Do I ask questions? *Yes.* Do I ask can I do anything to assist? *Yes.* Do I write up a formal observation on something so new to everyone? *No!* For example, years ago, we brought in a program called Math Their Way. One of the key components of the program was the use of manipulatives in the process. For the first month, we did nothing but let the kids play with the manipulatives. They got used to them and when it was time for the kids to use them for instructional purposes, they were a true educational tool and not a play thing. I utilize the same approach with teachers. When anything new comes into the district, it is hands-off for the first year. By hands-off I am referring to any *formal* observation or evaluation of a teacher utilizing the new product or initiative. This doesn't mean I am not present and sharing the new initiative, it just means *I am evaluating the initiative not the teacher*. This may not be the easiest thing to pull off but it is important.

Share-the-Wealth

One of the best ways to lead professional development is to recognize where great professional development should come from and how it works best. I am sure that there are many workshops and conferences that teachers can go to where they can attempt to improve their pedagogy. However, if properly established and with the proper collegial mindset, home grown is best!

I have effectively utilized a Share-the-Wealth program where building level administrators go into classrooms and cover for a teacher as he or she is partnering with another teacher in their classroom. Dual-teaching and/or observing that teacher is usually done and centers around a lesson and/or set of activities that the teacher-team has been working on. Honing a lesson down to improve student engagement, refining best practice and/or just the dialogue generated by two teachers working together in a classroom with kids in huge for professional development purposed.

Don't Let That Master Teacher Retire Just Yet [Grease Spot #24]

In ancient times and in not-so-ancient times but prior to the development and recording of the written word in tomes; history, lessons, and other important information was passed on, one person to another as people gathered together and listened to the advice of a sage. The written word allowed these teachings, rather than just being verbally passed from sage to neophyte, to be archived and referenced. The passing on of valuable information, the knowledge of a master teacher passed onto neophyte, was therefore venerated.

The apprenticeship program, as antiquated as it might appear at first blush, is still the best way to pass on skills and best practices. In our field we have student teaching and there are districts where Mentoring programs and Peer Coaching are effective. All are fine and do provide as close to an apprenticeship experience as our profession seemingly dares to nuzzle up to.

There is one singular and prolific fact that we all can agree on and yet we address in a less than robust fashion. Regardless of the texts, tools, computers, workbooks and SMART Boards that we place into our classrooms, nothing, *absolutely nothing* is more important than the person standing in the front of the classroom – the classroom teacher and his or her expertise. The focus of attention as well as the focus of dollars must be generated and placed on improving the productivity of classroom teachers. Absent that endeavor, children will be left behind and the race to the top will be over before the starting pistol is discharged.

Racing to the Top of What?

Now that we are all considering the Race To The Top, having just gotten used to not leaving any child behind, the flurry of new initiatives professed to solve the nation's educational woes points fingers and hangs the blade of the guillotine precariously over the heads of principals and teachers. The cries that *something must be done* is as ubiquitous and frequent as popcorn in a movie theater.

I have a proposal. Years ago, someone who I considered to be a master teacher announced her plans to retire at the conclusion of the school year. On the last day of school, she had finished giving all her files, master copies of dittos, old plan books, an assortment of lesson plans, classroom furniture, her beloved overhead, and easel to her colleagues. She, as had been ritualistically done in the past, passed on all of her worldly teaching accoutrements to those who would remain. She then turned and walked out of the building never to return again. She had passed on her written words and physical apparatus, her tomes of documented experiences. However, when she walked out the door, she took *the most important part* of her potential legacy and it was never shared – she took *how* she accomplished what she did out of the school.

What I consistently do not read about or hear in all the talk about improving schools is the value of master teachers working with novice and even experienced teachers. Wouldn't it be wonderful if a master teacher who was in their final year prior to retirement was not given classes to teach but was given (with full pay and full acquisition of seniority) the role of instructional specialist (sage). Now let me be perfectly blunt and clear; I am referring to a master teacher and not *every teacher* who is in their last year of teaching is a master teacher; hardly.

In my district, permanent substitute teachers come to school each day. On days when there is no one absent, I have these teachers cover, on a rotating basis throughout the day, the master teacher's class for an hour or two. Then, I place that master teacher in the classroom of a teacher who wants help with some aspect of classroom management or instruction. I have made it crystal clear to everyone that no one is being punished and it is not that I do not consider them to be excellent teachers in their own right. However, I do not want this *master teacher* only sharing her overhead projector and other assorted pedagogical paraphernalia as she walks out the door at the end of the school year. I want other teachers to sit in, watch, listen, and absorb the ethos that permeates the classroom. I want to set up conversations between them about great pedagogy as it is observed. Why should I be the only one, as principal, who regularly passes through that master teacher's room and be impressed and enlightened by what and how she does what she does?

With all of the money focused on so many programs, practices, incentives and assorted attempts to raise the achievement levels of students, the one glaring omission and the one that I believe would ultimately have the greatest impact is the effective use of master teachers as instructional specialists. The problem is that this process will take too long when measured against the need for instant, quick fixes fueled, many times, by political reasons. There is no gadgetry or new organizational strategy here, and that might not satisfy the attraction to novelty. It cannot be packaged and sold to benefit a textbook publisher who contributes to political campaigns. But I digress.

The money? Oh, yes the money! Districts will be a paying probably the highest paid teacher in the school (or district) to be out of a classroom and just teaching teachers! I can hear taxpayers shouting in unison, what a waste of funds! However, if appropriately viewed as a major professional development apparatus, in reality, this process will cost less than gearing up or bringing in new programs and the related costs of them. We would be taking the best of the best and allowing them to leave behind many of their skills that formally walked out the door with them!

Some will debate that we already have a program like this where veteran teachers serve as a supervisor for student teaching experiences, I would counter that while the student teacher experience is important and *somewhat* worthwhile, are student teachers always partnered with master teachers or are they with teachers who volunteer for the money or college credits that usually accompany supervising the student teacher? Also, can someone so brand new and totally inexperienced as a student teacher fully appreciate what a teaching supervisor has to offer at that time in the teacher training experience? I say no. Student teachers usually don't even know what they don't know or what they need to know, and be able to do. I submit that most don't even know the questions to ask. The unencumbered simplicity and beauty is that we are providing an avenue for master teachers to leave their legacy or at least exposing those remaining behind with their expertise and skill.

Since Socrates

What I am proposing is that the legacy of the slow and steady tortoise prevails over the expectations of the expedient hare. There are no quick fixes. If there were a special program or tool that would ensure that all kids would learn, someone since Socrates would have figured it out (packaged it, sold it, and be retired to a condo on the south coast of Maui).

Placing one-on-one professional development in the hands of those ex-traordinarily successful *master teachers*, who are in the best position to influence others, is an *invaluable commodity*. Want to improve instruction and positively influence student learning? Then seek out those *master teachers* in your school/school district and engage them in passing on their pedagogical legacy prior to them taking it with them into retirement.

Willing Teachers

Teachers are willing to share the large coffee pot perking in the faculty room but if that is all they share then a school is not functioning at its optimum level. The act of teachers teaching teachers is an art, a science, a process, a skill, and an indispensable component of building teacher capacity toward greatness. Unfortunately, in some cases, it can be just working towards plain competency. The ability of teachers to observe (in a formative, not summative manner) in order to learn from each other is a strong tenet of building teacher pedagogical capacity. Educational literature is replete with the tangible and highly positive benefits of colleagues sharing best practices, conferring about pedagogical issues, and building collegial partnerships; all geared towards improving in-struction.

Theory is theory but putting theory into practice is an issue that can prove to be slightly more difficult. When we seek lasting institute change, that becomes part of the culture of a school, the litmus test will always be if teachers see the change as *added value*. In such a case, the change endures. Lasting change takes at least three years to become part of the ethos and an ingrained practice of a school's staff but initially there must be a buy-in built on trust. How does the building principal create a culture where sharing-the-wealth of the staff is rudimentary and ongoing? Most importantly, what are those first steps toward building trust that is foundational to the sharing process?

As previously noted, the trust factor is huge when it comes to someone recognizing that they could benefit (and who couldn't) from sharing with a colleague. In this case, trust is the causative factor that allows teachers to take that crucial first step. You are asking teachers to open their classroom door to others and let other people in. In some schools this is tantamount to blasphemy. Certainly, conversations based upon pedagogical practices are exchanged between professionals at all hours of the school day. However, when does the conversation lead to *actual teacher visits* and *teacher observations* based upon what was discussed? When the trust factor is established and represents a constant thread in the tapestry of your school, will teachers step up and invite into their classroom settings a colleague who will sit and watch or team-teach with them?

You Have Something Important to Share

Will teachers be willing to share, colleague-to-colleague and not only over the communal coffee pot but on their home turf, their classrooms? Convincing certain people that they have something worth sharing is important. It has been my experience that *most great teachers do not realize how great they really are* and that, ironically, is because they have not witnessed others attempting to do what they do. Ideas, conceptual frameworks yet to be implemented, and methodologies that work well with a particular segment of the student population are great starting points.

There is a strong leadership component that must launch this sharing endeavor. Your request that each teacher select a buddy to share the wealth with during the school year is your first step. Creating a school master schedule where the teamed teachers have a common preparation time would be extremely helpful. But even if that is not possible, *you* must find the time in your schedule to support the effort. Your support as measured by the act of covering one teacher's class for an hour to allow that teacher to visit (I will not use the word *observe* because it has a negative connotation) and, subsequently, doing the same in a reciprocal act for the other teacher sends a strong, yet subliminal message of just how important this process is to you.

Once this ball starts to roll down the hill, teachers will, hopefully, see the value of having more than a common coffee pot and will embrace the concept of developing best practices *sans* formal documentation that is part of a supervision process. The dialogues germane to improving instruction continue in subsequent years when teachers rotate share the wealth partners and the building of teacher capacity is multiplied, *exponentially*. A faculty that has the kind of trust that will allow for this kind of sharing is a thriving and living entity. Your role as principal is to create a culture that will allow this to happen and this starts with building trust.

Motivation

As we all know, different people are motivated by different things. I have a cadre of teachers on a certain grade level who are constantly reinventing themselves by constantly revamping best practices, curricula focus and a how-could-we-have-taught-this-better mentality. *I have to run to keep up with them.* They are highly motivated and I do believe they feel fulfilled and consider themselves academic leaders. Yet others plug along with the word advancement only being connected to the next salary step. Ugh! Those who work for the pay rather than doing a job well are seldom effective.

As a profession, we are missing (editorial comment here) *professional steps.* Novice, Standard (not a good word here, please help me), and Master. It should be more than time in grade/department or college courses taken that would advance a teacher from one step to another step but rather by professional growth and ability. Salaries for beginning teachers should be at low, apprentice-subsistence levels. An apprentice-teacher *climbs* their way up the teaching ranks and earns a better salary by perfecting their ability level to teach. The salary line for a school district would remain constant based on what it is now because the lower, introductory salaries would be balanced by the higher salaries for master teachers. Teachers would have to demonstrate ability in order to advance in pay and they would not receive pay advancement based simply upon being in the job and receiving automatic pay increases. This will help to remove poor quality teachers from the system because they would be held to lower salaries and no increases until they improved. Health and medical insurances would be tied to this as would retirement benefits.

In Who Controls Teachers' Work? Power and Accountability in America's Schools, Richard Ingersoll (2003) stated that those who are entrusted with the training of this next generation are not entrusted with much control over many of the key decisions in their work. He goes on to say the result of this disenfranchising of teachers will be schools that de-professionalize and de-motivate teachers. Based upon this, it would seem wise to engage teachers in practices that motivate them. This requires teachers becoming increasingly empowered.

School systems have their own cultures and can be very different entities. I guess the first question you need to answer is whether the staff or individuals on staff have both the desire motivation and capacity to begin the process of shared leadership. It may be a concept that the staff needs to discuss and research to see the valuable for optimizing student learning. Most staff, in my experience, wants to be part of the academic decision-making that affects them. It serves as a motivator to have a degree of control over what you are doing.

I believe the second question deals with making sure we identify those staff members with the capacity. For example, staff members with great expertise in teaching writing could be engaged to share leadership responsibilities in this area. Richard DuFour noted that whenever anyone in the organization has a particular expertise to help solve a problem, he or she should emerge as the leader in that situation.

You need to know your staff members and their unique gifts and abilities [**Grease Spot #25**]. You would not, I suggest, engage staff members who are struggling to keep their heads above water. For example, you would not engage a person who demonstrates a lack of classroom management skills to a shared leadership role in the area of setting a discipline policy or in creating behavior intervention plans. In essence, as explained by Linda Darling Hammond (2010), "the principals job is to figure out what the strengths and interests of the other adults in the school are and use these strengths/weaknesses in ways that enhance the overall work of the school." It means identifying the weaknesses in your school where work can be accomplished by existing teacher capacity.

Roland Barth made a very famous analogy about a teacher-centered approach when he noted this statement about the advice given by airline cabin attendants: *In the unlikely event that an oxygen mask is needed and you are accompanied by a child, first put the mask on yourself and then on the child.* He then went on to state that teachers are able to best serve students when they themselves have been adequately served.

I have *played* this hand (the oxygen mask analogy) many times with my assistant superintendent, superintendent, PTA presidents, and other community organizations and even with my board of education because it rings so true to me. I always find it amazing how our educational stakeholders want taxpayer money going directly to the children! Many do not see the relationship between a highly trained instructional staff (and the $$$$ needed for that) and how that directly impacts students. There are none so blind as............

No principal can know the content of every academic discipline but you need to lead staff in identifying effective instructional philosophies, practices, methods, and strategies that will optimize learning and engage students metacognitively. I must admit that I really liked the statement, *guide on the side, not sage on the stage* to describe the principal's role in working with staff and bringing out their strengths. The phrase also made me chuckle given that when I entered the profession principals did pontificate from the stage like sages, but it never guaranteed what they had to say was wise but was rather more the result of exercising power. If we desire collaborative groups of professionals implementing inquiry to enhance their instructional practice to boost performance and achievement for all students, you must not act like the all-knowing principal. You must empower, facilitate, and invite teachers to act as professionals dedicated to continuous improvement.

Reforms coming from the top down do not have the same long-term sustainability as those coming from within the classroom [**Grease Spot #26**]. Teachers have seen many trends and swings of the pendulum from the top down and are eager to make decisions, find solutions, blaze a trail, and find themselves on the cutting edge when they see it is successful. There are always members of a staff who want to jump in early and others who wait to see if new approaches are successful. There are also those who need to be invited and encouraged. The key here is to build on existing strengths of your staff. The negative power of maintaining the status-quo is a significant grease spot on your high-wire [**Grease Spot #27**]. Simply seeking compliance is a great start and you can work on quality later as stakeholders get more comfortable.

I once had a teacher who was, on the surface, one you would think was very negative. He was the type of guy who noticed every flaw or potential flaw. I realized he had a gift for poring over data and statistics. When I invited him to help me collect and interpret the data on student writing prior to bringing it to staff, he jumped on it. Soon he was the data czar on staff with many peers asking for advice and interpretation. At the end of the day, he was one of the greatest supporters of new actions. What I am saying is; we, as principals, need to know the gifts and talents of individual staff members and invite them to be empowered and tap into their skill-sets.

Great leaders leave a host of new, motivated leaders as a legacy.

The Principal - Teacher Relationship: Leading from the Middle

Peter Northouse, in his book Leadership: Theory and Practice (2007), stated that studying the style approach of leaders determined that leadership is comprised of two kinds of behaviors: task and relationship behaviors. Task behaviors facilitate goal accomplishment by helping group members to achieve their objectives. Relationship behaviors help followers feel comfortable with themselves, with each other, and with the situation in which they find themselves. As a situational leader, there can be many times when you place yourself in the middle of the pack as you and the teachers assess, plan, and implement initiatives and/or strategies. The best principal-teacher relationships are developed when teachers realize that you are comfortable in your relationship with them as a leader and that you are *equally* as comfortable enabling teacher leaders around you.

In addition, sometimes a school has a mission and vision statement that is not founded upon reality or daily practice and are therefore, just lofty pronouncements that are neither measureable nor demonstrable. Often I think that most mission statements focus on student learning - which I believe is good - but do not really focus on *teacher learning* other than merely mentioning the words *a learning community* and a belief statement where staff takes responsibility for student learning through collaboration, data analysis, research and a willingness to modify or adapt practice to improve pupil performance. Your mission must include teacher education and to build their capacity.

Effective teaching occurs when teachers are successful *leaders* for their students. Just as teachers follow and are guided by administrators, students look up to the teacher to motivate, drive, and teach them. Effective teaching (just like educational leadership) begins with forming relationships, making connections, creating opportunities, gaining trust, and of course, listening. It is fascinating to me how the both relationships (principal-teacher and teacher-student) relate similarly and are interdependent.

Chapter 4

Observation and Evaluation

I always feel there is something I can learn every day from observing teachers.

As I reflect on the literature that I have read about the evaluation process for teachers and factoring in my experiences, I conclude that the most challenging aspect of evaluation for principals would be developing a technique and the skill sets for effectively observing. I view observing as the act of recognizing and noting facts or an occurrence using one or more of my senses. *Observing* is recognizing and noting details, and *evaluating* is deciding which details matter and which are not so important. Because the process of observing is pure subjectivity, the results of an observation can be arguable because interpretations can vary. This is why your fact gathering process is so important. It serves to support the context in which you are observing (both formally and informally).

There is a judgment factor upon which on an observation/evaluation is based. There is a pedagogical philosophy that the evaluator brings to the process. You cannot allow for the possibility that the determinations made cannot be supported by the *facts* of the observation. The question for any principal is *how do you develop a process of observing and then concluding an objective decision from what has been seen and heard?*

I am inclined to believe that teachers get better with guidance rather than by the mere accumulation of time and the experiences of doing the same things - sometimes wrong, over and over again. I have observed many teachers whose pedagogical approach to teaching shows that they have not made any progress since their first year of teaching. I see teachers who never utilize strategies for making their lessons exciting and creative. Their belief is a malaise of it worked ten years ago, so it will work this year as well. The observation process can, at times, be internalized by the teacher as *just let me get this done*. The truth is that *some* teachers will not change just because of time unless someone with greater skills assists them in pedagogical growth.

There is a thought that each teacher sees themselves as an *independent contractor* when it comes to the act of teaching even though they are represented by a union and there is one contract, the same contract, for everyone. This feeling of autonomy/independence – I close my classroom door and do what I want – is the antithesis of what a collaborative, creative, and effective faculty should be in terms of instruction. While most teachers will buy into a prescribed and preset set of curricula, the same sense of sharing and consistency is totally lost when it comes to pedagogy.

Just the Facts

The act and responsibility of conducting supervision of teachers is an easily greased area of your high-wire [**Grease Spot #28**]. There is, of course, no way around this critically important endeavor. It is your responsibility, as principal, to utilize supervision of instruction as a way to improve instructional pedagogy and, *I am speaking realistically here*, to remove personal who are not *highly qualified* to teach. It is the process that you utilize that will determine whether or not your high-wire is greased. O.K., time to shoot myself in the foot! I have come to realize and I want to share with you a simple fact that has taken me thirty-plus years to learn. I will pass this on to you because I am hopeful you will learn this sooner rather than later. Given the laws that support teachers with tenure in most states, it is darn near impossible to have a tenured teacher removed (fired for classroom incompetency). You have a better chance of them robbing a bank in Times Square at noon with over 1,000 witnesses and once captured and convicted, that is how they will be let go. In reality (and with the continued use of my theft metaphor) they are committing highway robbery by accepting money for doing a job they are so poor at and we, all administrators, are complicit because there is no expedient manner to remove ineffective teachers. Having said that, and living with my hiring mistakes, I give you a piece of sage advice. If, in the first two years, a new teacher does not *impress the socks off of you* - let them go – *fire them!* There, I wrote it for all to read.

Realistically, who wants to be observed - no one! No one wants someone watching what they are doing and inevitably making a judgment about the quality of their work. Yet, in private industry, this happens all the time. If you are working for General Motors and are putting on lug nuts to hold the wheels on a car, and as the car rolls off the assembly line, the tires consistently fall off, reality is that you will no longer be working for General Motors. Why should we, as educators, be any different? Who the heck gets paid and gets yearly wage increases not based upon improvement or highly effective performance but rather simply on seniority and longevity. *It makes no sense!*

If there are obvious components of a teacher's job performance that are not acceptable, what do you do? Should a teacher who is not productive be allowed to continue and the answer to that question would be yes because they have tenure! *Tenure provides an ability to develop and maintain incompetency and still be employed.* The difficult concept and reality here is you do not see the metaphorical tire falling off right away. How do you really *measure* the progress of students and, more importantly, how did the teacher's performance enter into and/or cause the results?

If the lug nuts were not made properly or the threads on the tire mounts were equally poorly made, and the worker was securing them as he or she was training; then one could surmise that the worker should not be let go. It was not his or her fault. We are now heading down a very dangerous road because to what degree is the capability and/or potential ability of the children in the class impacting on your judgment about the teacher? The child sitting in class not willing to participate because he or she sees no use for Algebra relevant to the world they know is whose fault? A child whose inability to cognitively focus and understand concepts will obviously do poorly regardless of the pedagogy employed by the classroom teacher. Then what?

Reality Check

The reality of your high-wire is that anyone and everyone proving residency within your community and even those homeless and living under the train overpass within your community catchment area, are coming to your school. You and your teachers will be judged by how *every* child who walks through your doorway succeeds *regardless* of their social and emotional needs, desires, preparation for the grade level course and/or existing disabilities that interfere with their education.

It is almost un-American to indicate that some children could have less ability than others. That is why it is the belief of every politician that *every* student, in *every* school, should go to college and that it is the responsibility of the classroom teachers (and principals) to ensure that they have the skills to go to college - and if not, there is something wrong with the teacher (and principal). I have never heard a politician *ever* talk about *parent responsibility*, thereby, putting the onus where it really belongs. Egalitarian Americans do not like to say or hear that someone is not college material. And yet there are dozens and dozens of students graduating from every high school in the country who will make an excellent life for themselves and their families as plumbers, air conditioning and heating experts, automobile mechanics, chefs (my son), landscapers, carpenters, and hundreds of other skilled trades. Many visual learners simply do not learn from books. They learn from technical diagrams or images or on-the-job experiences. Who is to say that kind of learning is lesser than another kind or that those people are not as smart as those with a college degree?

It has come down to the concept that no one is looking at the lug nut or the threaded spoke for possible reasons as to why the wheels keep falling off. No, it is the worker's fault that the tires keep falling off. So, if the assessment scores are not high enough, fire the teacher and the principal! Now there is a real rational decision on the part of politicians! My question is, once fired, who will replace them and won't the cycle just continue with a new set of names and faces but the same potential causative factor – the parents and the kids!?

Having established the concept that every child sent to us as educators is not perfect and will not respond the way we want, we can now move onto the act of delivering instruction. Because, with all due respect to the children that come our way with a myriad of problems and issues, there are, of course, educators who should not be in the classroom if they are going to continue to deliver instruction in the manner that they always have been. Enter you the principal, stage right and, by the way, watch out for the grease!

I believe approximately eight to eleven *percent* of the teachers in *every school* across the country are bordering on incompetency, and if given the opportunity to remove each one of them on Friday afternoon, Monday morning would be a better day for the school and the students in their classes. This, of course, assumes that you, as principal, are competent enough to hire a better teacher than the one you just let go.

The first question then becomes, is it your responsibility to teach teachers how to teach? Didn't the college and/or university they graduated from only graduate the *best teachers* and didn't it *only grant a degree* to those who could teach effectively? Didn't your state's Department of Education *only grant a teaching license* to those individuals who are *highly qualified* to teach? Reality is that the state gives a license to anyone who graduated from an accredited university. The irony here is that the same governing body, the State Education Department that grants a certificate to teach is the same department now creating assessments of students' performance and utilizing those results to measure teacher performance with the intent to remove ineffective teachers! The same teachers they indicated were effective by granting them a license! Wouldn't it have been better for the students in schools across your state to not have granted a license in the first place to incompetent teachers? Am I missing something here!?! *What is wrong with this picture?* Why not develop a system where we put *every* graduate in a classroom with kids, and let's see if they can do the job *prior to licensing!*

Supervision of Instruction

I think that supervision can take on two separate roles dependent upon whether or not you are in an elementary or secondary school. Elementary school principals have a more complex responsibility in that there are no department chairpeople who serve in the role of curriculum experts [department chairs, lead teachers, directors]. Elementary principals have to be the expert in all curriculum areas while their secondary counterparts have area experts to consult with and rely on. The role of supervision of instruction on the elementary level spans the gamut of pedagogy and content while the secondary level administrator can place most of the effort and focus on pedagogy. The elementary principal needs to be the curriculum expert in all curricula areas. This requires his or her continual research and improvement of their academic and pedagogical knowledge and skills so that effective instruction can occur.

So after establishing your responsibility in terms of the variety of support you may or may not have, how do you build an ethos within the school that allows teachers to be collaborative partners in their own *improvement?* Teachers should have access to up-to-date curricula resources. This does not mean using the latest cannot miss methodology to teach a specific curriculum needs to be always updated. There will always be the latest and greatest way to teach a certain subject. This occurs most often in the areas of reading and writing where the *new* method seems to change with the season.

There is a good chance you will lose the cooperation and support of the faculty if each year or so you present the newer method at the expense of the older one. If seems to me that if there was one best way to teach a certain curriculum area, it would have been discovered long ago. You grease your own high-wire [**Grease Spot #29**] if you keep on changing horses. One suggestion is not to completely disavow the newest methodology but rather maintain an open mind and set of eyes to anything new and listen to your master teachers.

The Baby and the Bath Water Thing

I have always presented the *latest* as simply the *newest* addition to our smorgasbord of pedagogical options. As you walk down the smorgasbord, look and see what appears to be most effective *for your target population*. Always remember your target population comes first, long before you jump onto the latest educational bandwagon of the hottest new teaching method. I have always allowed teachers to select what segments of an initiative works best. We never threw out our basal readers when the whole language movement surfaced. In fact, the whole language movement forced the textbook publishers to create better basal readers. We still use a phonics approach when necessary - and that is the key. An eclectic approach to education opens the smorgasbord to utilize what is best and *most effective for your kids*. This doesn't mean what is easiest for the teachers to teach or the one they like the best. The method of choice can only be *and must always be* what works best for your target population.

When teachers know your focus will always be on the kids, then they will be more willing to open their minds to new things. You are not mandating you are looking. You are not jumping onto the latest bandwagon you are simply keeping your eyes open to what is new in the field and adapting what might work best for your kids. Our eclectic approach helps to serve all of our kids. It is always best to utilize as many *Response to Intervention* practices that we can utilize in order to try and support student effort.

The link must always be maintained between improvement of instruction and professional development for teachers. How do you take the emotionally charged aspect of teacher observation and step into the realm of professional development? Remember, even in the most open of venues, teachers will see observation as a judgment of their performance. How you make the transition from performance evaluation to professional development for the good of kids, will separate you from other principals and will serve to move your school forward.

How do you make the separation between supporter of professional development for teachers and an evaluator of performance? I think it is important to take stock of your faculty. Who appears to be an outstanding educator and who are just competent? Next, there will be that segment of the faculty who are incompetent and require *a great* deal of your time. You will need to determine just *how bad is bad* and what you will need to do to either assist in correcting the deficits or monitoring them so that it does not get any worse. And here is where we lose most lay people. The process to fire (yes, I used the f-word) a tenured teacher is nearly impossible to complete and can be an extremely expensive process for a school district. Why? After all, demonstrated incompetence is demonstrated incompetence! Why not ask the teacher to find another place to work? Unfortunately, as previously noted, the educational and teacher licensing system does not work that way and then there is the teachers' union protecting its weakest teacher. Protect your weakest and you protect everyone!

Time Poverty

So, now you have a decision given the amount of time you have to spend on pedagogy. Do you work to support the accomplished teachers, work to build up the competent teachers, or work toward overcoming the deficits of the incompetents? On the secondary level you might have more options because you have more people to assist you in the area of curriculum and instruction (department chairs, district directors). There is no one answer because every school is different but realize that whichever groups you service to the lesser degree, creates grease on the high-wire [**Grease Spot #30**]. This is one of those situations where no matter what group you step towards, you are taking an equal step in the opposite direction away from others. You cannot be in two places at one time.

How do you service those teachers who are doing an extraordinary job? You cannot forget those teachers. While at first blush it appears they will be fine on their own and you can concentrate on the others, remember these are the people who are setting the pace. They are the ones carrying the standard and the yardstick that all others will be measured by. They are the ones that are probably teaching your toughest courses and your best and brightest kids as well as your neediest kids. These teachers need just as much support as the others. No one wants to feel they are doing a great job and are going unnoticed! If they are the ones who you expect to lead others, they cannot be left unnoticed, unappreciated, and unsupported.

How about the competent teachers? Well, do you want to go to a *competent* doctor or a *competent* attorney or a *competent* financial planner? In some ways, these are the teachers who will probably make up the largest segment of your teacher population. It is easy to slip from competent to incompetent and you need to fully support the teachers you want to make *extraordinary*. These are the teachers who can really benefit from professional development opportunities. They also benefit from working with other teachers, especially those extraordinary teachers.

The incompetent teachers are easily to recognize. They will be instantly recognized by you when you see them teaching (or, in this case, attempting to teach). They will be the reason the phone will ring and will be the source of student complaints on a regular basis. How much time can you afford to spend in the classroom of those teachers? How much time do you have to meet with the teacher to address your concerns and the concerns of others? Here is where the secondary principal might have more corporate time available; meaning more people to work with the teacher than the sole administrator in an elementary school.

Where to Start

Approaching the teacher in need of improvement starts with a focus on what is or what is not occurring in the classroom. Can you and the teacher come to consensus that there needs to be improvement? Start with small issues and things that can be easily addressed. You will need to demonstrate that there is an issue and in many cases you need to prove to the teacher that there is an issue. You will be amazed at some teachers who cannot see the forest because the trees are in the way. You might have to write down what the teacher has said or did in the classroom, so you can specifically point to the situation, "remember when Bob did (this) and you did that? I think it would have been more effective if you had..." If there are classroom management issues, then suggestions that focus on specific issues or children that might be causing the situation will be valid. The ineffective teacher whose students have poor retention, poor test scores, or poor - everything; most probably has poor classroom management skills as well.

I would look for professional development opportunities that would allow *teams* of teachers to be trained at the same time in areas like instruction data mining and interpretation, as well as curriculum design. I would also invest some time in training that supports groups of teachers on *how to become teams* and *how teams function effectively*. You need to fully buy into the concept of when *educators learn, students learn*. "Every student deserves to experience great teaching every day. And yet, there are still schools in which some students experience extraordinary teaching while others in classrooms next door or down the hall experience less effective teaching. When educators collaborate, they have opportunities to share strengths and seek guidance from colleagues. When teachers collaborate to plan lessons and assessments, students in the same course benefit from the collective expertise of all the teachers of that course. In schools where collaboration among educators is routine, great teaching becomes a reality for every student in every classroom" (Hirsch and Killion, 2009, p.464).

Think about the following if you will and for your consideration. As you look around your school at those teacher-leaders - where did they get their leadership crown from? Were they anointed by administration, did they stand still when everyone else in the department/grade level took a step back, were they singled out because everyone saw them as a teacher-of-choice, or did they step up to the plate? And, most importantly, what was or will be your role in this process?

Would it be wrong to have expectations about the observation and evaluation process that the teacher should take responsibility for his/her professional performance and growth? Reflective teachers do not wait for observation or evaluation by the principal to determine the areas of strengths and weaknesses in their professional practice. The principal should be invited as coach to guide and provide feedback through observation with formative assessment. That way, the process is viewed as collaborative and helping rather than monitoring and controlling. What you do and say will help to create this kind of culture for your school.

Carpooling

Goleman, et al. (2002) maintained that, "When people feel good, they work at their best. Feeling good lubricates mental efficiency, making people better at understanding information and using decision rules in complex judgments, as well as more flexible in their thinking. Upbeat moods, research verifies, make people view others or events in a more positive light. That in turn helps people feel more optimistic about their ability to achieve a goal, enhances creativity and decision making skills, and predisposes people to be helpful" (p.14). Placing teachers in leadership roles throughout the building will serve you well. Having the right person in the right place at the right time is all you have to figure out to make this successful.

Carpooling (TEAM building) is a process. Recognizing that there are leadership qualities within members of the faculty and having the guts to use them wisely is the trick. Allowing others to lead is at times relinquishing power. You need to ask yourself, honestly; if someone else had accomplished this, how would I feel about it? I have found that the more power that you give away the more ultimately comes back to you.

One of the first things in the process of developing a TEAM approach is understand yourself and how *you fit* into a TEAM. In the past, what role have you played in groups? How were the roles developed in these groupings in terms of who performed what job? Is there any specific strength that you personally brought to these groups? Is there any consistency that you can see in hindsight? Did you consistently have the same role? The most successful leaders are those who have learned to follow and, subsequently, when asked to lead, disperse power among competent stakeholders.

The question you must ask yourself would be did *your involvement* in these groups help or hinder the group from attaining its mission? Paraphrasing Groucho Marx: *Would you want to be a member of any group that would have someone like you as a member?* Now ask yourself, why? Now that you have been honest, what do you need to change that would make *you* a better group member?

O.K., up off the couch, the therapy session is over. Now that you have examined yourself as part of a TEAM, you will be better prepared to make selections or support participation by others in TEAMS that will benefit your school.

Another way to help ensure the effectiveness of instruction in every classroom is to develop a common language of instruction that is universally known, understood, and utilized by you and your faculty. Once that common pedagogical language is applied, the next step is to develop a common and consistently utilized vocabulary presented to students as they pass through elementary grade levels and specific courses in the secondary complex. So now you have a common pedagogical vocabulary used by teachers and a common and consistent academic vocabulary of critical terms utilized for students.

This commonality endeavor helps to eradicate any systems level problems and serves to thwart any classroom teacher level issues, or at the very least gets everyone on the same page in terms of terminology. It is amazing how these two simple steps serve as huge first steps toward collaboration, shared ideas, and movement in a common direction. It also serves to create what Marzano refers to as a highly reliable school.

Choosing Up Sides

The high-wire is a grease trap [**Grease Spot #31**] of unfulfilled expectations of TEAM approaches to solving problems locally and district-wide. Teachers want to make decisions about their work place and you should provide them with opportunities. While it is not a great practice for you to make isolated decisions on your own, so too is it wrong and counter-productive to give individual teachers that power as well. Therefore, the TEAM concept is born and is the mother of necessity.

In addition to the many productive members of any group there are those who are always late, are never prepared, and/or make little or no real contribution to the TEAM. And, at the same time, they want to become a member, in good standing, of your TEAM. These are the people that are *carried* across the finish line and get credit (but did little or nothing).

In the classes I teach in educational administration, I regularly try this little experiment. I randomly divide the class into teams of six people. I tell the class prior to randomly dividing them that we have a *large* and *significant* project due the last week of the class and I want them to conduct a four minute, pre-planning session for this project. I inform them that at the end of four minutes, they need to come back to the class and each team will have selected:

One member to serve as the sole voice of the team.

One member to serve as a back-up if the leader is not in class.

One person will record (a secretary) the minutes of the team meetings which will be submitted to me at the end of each team project.

One member to serve as the *runner* to get any supplies that the team might need.

I also inform them that everyone on the team will receive the same grade.

Obviously, in a group of six, two people will have nothing assigned to them. If I have five groups in the class, I pull five people aside prior to the start of the class the day when the groups are assigned and assign one person to *watch* a group and to note the dynamics of the work of the group during the process of selecting people for the roles noted above.

In most cases, the group selection process works as follows:

1. No one wants to be the secretary. The secretary has too much work and there is the fear of making spelling errors.

2. One person will volunteer to serve as spokesperson. This usually happens either because someone is a natural leader and always takes over or someone panics because the group has already used up three and a half minutes of the allotted four minutes.

3. One of the lazier people usually volunteers to be the *runner* because you have a job but it really is not that important of a job *and* you cannot be anything on the team that you do not want to be.

4. There will be people who just sit there (usually with their arms folded across their chest) and say nothing. They do not volunteer or suggest who should lead or how to go about the process of selecting a leader, fearing that opening their mouth will result in leadership being thrust upon them.

My point to the class as we reassemble and the *observers* report the dynamics of what each group went through is that this will be a microcosm of a school faculty. All of the behavior patterns within this exercise will be present. You will need to make sure that the right people are in the right places, so that the group activity for your school can move forward and come to a successful fruition. Always recognize at the start of any group endeavor that there will be natural leaders and there will be natural arm folded slackers.

Great Collaboration

A good leader encourages collaboration and participation in decision-making among the staff members. There are many good teachers that have great, innovative ideas that can enhance the school environment. When teachers see that their suggestions are utilized, their confidence is boosted and they feel valued. To ensure a positive learning environment, a good leader provides an opportunity and arena for ideas to be shared and discussed among all stakeholders involved in the academic progress of students. As leaders, we need to encourage those who work with us to continue to grow and improve.

Your TEAM leaders within your school must be people who bring to the group strong interpersonal skills, good communication skills, and are highly productive problem solvers. They must also be people who others would want to follow. Many of these people could easily rival the current principal but for one reason or another they do not want to be a principal, they prefer to remain in the classroom. That is great! Give them all the academic leadership they want and *count your blessings!* The concept of mutual respect in any educational environment feeds the concept of input and growth through the delivery of diverse opinions, which in turn allows everyone to stretch and grow. I love it when diverse opinions clash and an intense dialogue emerges. It is the *juice* that allows the mind to grow.

The characteristics of a great collaborative effort are:

1. A high level of interdependence among members.

2. The principal *is a member* of the TEAM and knows how to use power.

3. Each member is willing and is able to contribute.

4. A relaxed climate for communication is present even when *you* are in the room.

5. Members have mutual *trust* (I think I have referred to this word previously).

6. People are prepared to take risks.

7. The TEAM is clear about goals.

8. Members can disagree without personal attacks.

9. The TEAM has the capacity to create new ideas.

Community of Learners

A school culture that invites teachers, students, parents and administrators to become an effective community of learners looks like a mini-society that empowers stakeholders to be participants in the educational process. That community of learners looks like what John Dewey (1933) might describe as an *empowered* organization. In this community, teachers, parents, and students would all be called upon to make decisions by participating in the evidence gathering process. It would not be a *top down* organization, but one where the people on the front lines would be enlisted to decide what was best for the community of learners.

An organization that operates by these principles practices subsidiarity: the belief that any activity that can be done by a less centralized entity should be. There is no question as to the relevance of allowing teachers and staff members to do their jobs without interference from administrators. There is also no question about the firsthand knowledge and experience that teachers and staff have that makes them eminently more qualified to handle most issues and problems and make decisions.

The principal acts as an advisor to others in the educational community. The empowered community allows teachers the time and information to make decisions. Students and parents in this type of culture would also be provided with levels of decision making privileges. *Everybody has a part in decision-making*

As silly and irrelevant as it might appear at first blush, some schools have formed committees to develop culture. They collect data and implement strategies to improve the school's culture. They determine what is hindering the school from having a unifying, positive identity as well as figuring out what will lead to improvement and the subsequent monitoring of their success. These groups understand the role of culture in supporting student success. I believe there are ways to draw people in. Often times, people do not jump in as the concept of shared leadership is new to them, they lack confidence or maybe they just have a bad attitude and do not want to be collaborative. These are usually the people who, as they are saying hello to you each morning, add, "Well, only eighteen more days until our next vacation." That simple, seemingly innocent (and even could be considered as a funny) comment *is a disease* that you do not want spread throughout your school. Those people who are living merely from vacation to vacation (and that is their incentive to move forward) should be working at Disney World, not in your school.

Additionally, there are staff members who will sit back to see how all this works before they jump on board as these teachers have seen many things come and go during their career. *This is O.K.* and their tentative nature should be respected. Starting with a small group and sharing your success with other teachers also lights a flame and encourages the more reluctant to join if they see the success as well as effective decisions being made. *Be willing to give them time.*

Consensus Building [Grease Spot #32]

Please let me expand on consensus building that I touched upon in Chapter 3. As principal, consensus building is a problem solving strategy that could be used to address one or more sources of tension and conflict within a school. This strategy deals with resolving conflicts and involves the opposing groups in trying to find solutions that are mutually acceptable. You must understand the importance of consensus building because many problems arise when there is a diverse school population and it affects their interests which are inter-connected. These problems affect the group as a whole and in order to resolve it, both groups must work together. It is extremely difficult and often ineffective and counterproductive for principals to try to solve problems by imposing a solution because this is rarely successful.

Consensus building offers a way for diverse stakeholder groups to solve problems in ways that are acceptable to all. It permits groups to contribute to the decision-making processes, rather than leaving decisions up to a single, select group or person. When decisions are made sans consensus, it is possible for one stakeholder group to be unhappy and this considerably slows the implementation of the decision. While consensus building may take time, it *develops* solutions.

The process of consensus building helps to establish a common framework for developing a solution that works for everyone. The process also encourages groups to explore integrative solutions and allows them to deal with issues that are related in an open forum. Trade-offs and developed solutions will meet needs more completely than if decisions are imposed on stakeholders and the process does not call for stakeholder participation.

One of the possible hurdles that may arise when implementing consensus building to resolve conflicts is the inability of the teachers to be effective mediators. Teachers should develop the skills to build consensus through facilitating conflict resolution. Convey, (1994) notes, that in order for a TEAM to be successful, it is essential that members know the basics of conflict resolution, delegation, and consensus building. When teachers lack these skills or are unable to implement the decision that has been agreed upon then it might give rise to additional conflicts. When bringing a TEAM together teachers should be informed in the basics of the process of consensus building. The principal is the foundation for moving forward a process by which the conflicting stakeholder groups can effectively work through to find a solution.

Follow My Lead but Don't be Afraid to Speak Up

Having a strong philosophy on leadership directly correlates with one's ability to lead consistently and successfully via the mutual respect grown out of strong relationships. Everyone has a core set of beliefs by which they base their decision-making process upon. It is vitally important to the TEAM that effective collaboration takes place between all of the team's members. G.A. Donaldson wrote that good leadership is *invitational* leadership. It will be you, the building principal, who should invite others to be leaders too. Allowing each individual an opportunity to voice their ideas and concerns builds trust and can help to unify the team. Creating a culture of success through establishing quality relationships is essential in building a quality TEAM of stakeholders.

Successful principals incorporate a leadership style that aligns with their vision and actions. For this reason, principals are the change agents within schools to motivate and unite followers to achieve foundational objectives. Furthermore, you must see yourself as and be a solid contributor to the development of the *work culture* within your school by upholding teacher capacity to create successful growth. This is accomplished by developing a leadership mantra that is supported by your actions - *you* are the hardest worker by your actions and deeds and not by telling everyone how hard you are working.

lead by example

You will need to develop a sense of the use of *positional* and *personal* power. The power of position is the easy one; you are given that by the fact you were hired to lead. A great leader knows how to lead and how to support their staff to provide an environment that they can grow in. A leader is able to motivate staff and values their opinions (personal power) as well as seeks out their opinion. A good leader is willing to take the risk to have others give input to provide solutions.

Shared Leadership
Sharing the Road Map for Traversing the High-Wire

As noted earlier, I believe that the degree to which we promote shared leadership must vary with existing conditions within your school. This being postulated, it must be your goal to promote shared responsibility recognizing this is a process that begins with you believing in it.

The first question you need to answer is whether the members of the staff have both the desire and capacity to begin the process of shared leadership. It may be a concept the staff needs to discuss and research to see if they see it as valuable for optimizing student learning. Most staffs, in my experience, want to be part of the decision-making that affects them. I believe the second question deals with making sure we identify those staff members with the capacity to build successful shared leadership TEAMS. In addition to the data czar I wrote about earlier, a staff member with expertise in teaching writing could be engaged to share leadership in this area. Whenever anyone in the organization has a particular expertise to help solve a problem, they should emerge as the leader in that situation.

You would not, I suggest, engage staff who are struggling to keep their heads above water. For example, you would not engage a person who demonstrates a lack of classroom management skills to a shared leadership role in the area of setting a discipline policy or in creating behavior intervention planning. In essence, the principal's job is to figure out what the strengths and interests of the other adults in the school are and use these strengths and interests in ways that enhance the school. It also means identifying the weaknesses in the school where work can be accomplished by building faculty capacity.

Although buy-in is important to shared leadership, it is also important to realize that it is possible to have staff members that never buy-in or never volunteer. Ultimately, one wants a school staff where all stakeholders share responsibility for students and are willing to create the conditions where all are successful. This means the process of shared leadership must expand to create a condition where all staff are engaged, volunteering and participating to varying degrees. Easily written, now go out and try and do it!

While trust is an important variable as in promoting a culture of trust, it must be said that trust is also developed when staff is given the opportunity to gain experience with shared leadership. Even when shared leadership results in failure, this can also be a stepping-stone to success. Sometimes we make mistakes and need to learn through trial and error, like any scientific practitioner. This can be part of the norms or parameters identified for such shared leadership groups.

I believe that the degree to which we promote shared leadership must vary with existing conditions within your school. This being stated, it must be your goal to promote shared responsibility recognizing this is a process, a process beginning with you believing in the concept.

If you are new to a school with little or no experience with shared leadership, you must spend time getting to know your staff and their specific capabilities and the general needs of the school before charging ahead. With this being said, it seems that you could begin slowly with an area like discipline in the hallways or cafeteria, which are areas that involve all staff, with an aim to being successful and spreading the practice of shared leadership.

Jigsaw Puzzle

It is realistic to equate a faculty and their relationship to the accomplishment of all goals and initiatives as a huge jigsaw puzzle and each and every member of your staff (including yourself as principal) is one piece of that puzzle. Imagine, if you will, that you have a combined certificated and non-certificated staff of 150 people. You now have a one hundred and fifty piece puzzle that must be put together for just about every decision, initiative, and/or issue.

There is a need to build up a collaborative system by sharing and assigning tasks. Each person could work on different topics or lessons. The whole job is completed by putting together all the individual pieces. This is a jigsaw puzzle approach of cooperation. By doing so, each member develops a sense of shared responsibility instead of over-relying on the work of others.

I Am Not the Instructional Leader of My School and I Planned it that Way

During the past few years, I have been increasingly reflective of my role as principal and the road I have traveled upon. At this point in my career, I can see less miles ahead of me than behind me. I have observed and pondered, reflected and then assessed what I see when I look back. I have also planned how I want to traverse the few miles remaining ahead of me. The requirements of serving as a mentor to less experienced principals and my facilitating educational leadership classes at a local university have resulted in the need to analyze what I do and how I do what I do within the school where I am principal. My mentees and college level students, all of whom are teachers seeking to become administrators, have asked about instructional leadership and how to best attain the role of a school's instructional leader. There isn't a piece of educational literature that does not ascend the school principal to the position of instructional leader. And there will not be an interview that aspiring principals will have that will not ask them to describe how they would function as *the* instructional leader of a school.

Never Was, Never Should Have Been

The school that I have been honored to lead for the past thirty-two years as principal has won both state and national honors for excellence and our student assessment scores in English Language Arts, Math, Science, and Social Studies are extremely high. I have also been honored as the New York State Elementary School Principal of the Year (2009) and also recognized as a National Distinguished Principal that year as well. Having established that as a baseline, I am the first to admit *and proudly*, that I am not the instructional leader of the school, I am *one of* the instructional leaders. I am plain and simple, the *instructional manager.* I will not enter into the fray of discourse concerning leader versus manager. What I will offer, however, is the concept that creating a cadre of outstanding teachers who understand how kids learn best, produces the school's instructional leaders. These extraordinary teachers create and share best practices within the ethos created by the building principal that provides those closest to the students with decision-making abilities about curriculum content and sequencing as well as the implementation of best practices. These are the people who advise *this* instructional manager about necessary instructional changes. The ratio of instructional leaders to instructional manager can easily be 15 to 1 in a school of 45 to 50 full- and part-time teachers. I operationally realize that not everyone can be or should be an instructional leader and I, as the instructional manager, recognize and embrace this fact.

Asking the Correct Managerial Questions as a Leader

To follow this philosophy does not mean I have abandoned my role as leader. A leader must be visible in classrooms observing lesson both formally and informally and seeing whether those lessons engage students. I find myself looking at students and their outcomes first, and I am influenced by those outcomes. A leader asks questions utilizing words such as *why, when, what,* and *how.* These inquisitive words are foundational to management decisions and serve to probe when they are part of questions such as:

Why are you teaching this?

When is the best time (of day, grade, in the school year) to teach this?

What are the best methodologies to present this information?

What should our assessments look like?

What should be our intervention strategies?

Again, the primary and foundational component of the principles of instructional management is *trust.* When teachers know that *they* drive instruction, there is a mindset of establishing the *important* work that needs to be accomplished. Because the work is teacher derived, child centered, and outcomes driven teachers feel great about what they are accomplishing. The wheel is then perpetually turning under your guidance and management (and I'll even let you call it leadership, if that makes you feel better). Teachers *trust* me to support their needs, and I *trust* them to be on the front lines and to know, develop, and successfully implement what works best for our kids.

My Role

Having the discipline and courage to cull out those teachers who are not performing well prior to granting tenure creates a comfort zone for me and enthusiastically allows me to hand over the reins of real instructional leadership. Outstanding teachers want outstanding teachers teaching on their grade level or in their department, in their school and in the classroom next to them. There is only one reason for a poor quality teacher and that is a poor quality principal who hired and, subsequently, maintains that teacher. That is my job and yes, it is a management function. I also know that it provides a sense of stability for the faculty. Also, teachers know that I do not insist that we hop onto every trendy, pedagogical bandwagon that heads down Education Highway. They know I turn to them, as instructional leaders, for advice, consult, and direction at those times.

I am in classrooms daily, but, the last time I was in a classroom teaching for an entire school year was more than thirty-four years ago. How could I possibly be *the instructional leader* when I have not been in the trenches for thirty-four years? I have charted our course and manage the day-to-day functioning via feedback from those who have contact with students *every day*. When teachers see their principal as recognizing and valuing their skills and input toward the betterment of the students and the school at-large, it creates an environment where the management-leadership role becomes secondary to the importance of student success. I have many instructional leaders within the school and only one instructional manager - and it works.

Donuts and "Oh, I Once Spilled My Coffee" Meetings

One of the most slippery areas on the high-wire [**Grease Spot #33**] is your relationship with your faculty. I will wax philosophical in the coming pages and, at times, I will get down and a little dirty. Because while there is an infinite number of right and wrong ways of leading a group of professionals, there are as many factors that distinguish one group of teachers from another that makes no process or idea universal in its acceptance, workability or inability. All I can do is cast a few thoughts out upon the water and just pick the one or two that floats *your* boat. However, please be aware that each of your encounters with faculty can easily become a slippery spot on your high-wire.

Adult learning is extremely different from child or young adult learning. A teacher is expected to know everything because he or she is, well, a teacher! Students, and most parents, hold them in high regard because of their education and pedagogical abilities. Day-in and day-out they are the ones with the answers. Day-in and day-out their expertise goes almost unquestioned by their students. They are sages, and the more advanced in years on the job they become, the more sage-like they become - *and see themselves.*

Now try teaching these veteran dogs (and I use the term *endearingly*) new tricks. This, at the same time, becomes a sad situation because everyone can still learn something. The sharing of best practices in an educational setting is a growth potential that every sage (teacher) *should* enjoy, relish, and look forward to on a yearly basis (key functional word here is *should*). At times, you will think that not only is the high-wire greasy but that it has been significantly raised at the end toward which you are walking. Not every teacher thinks he or she requires new tricks. Personally, I believe a little bit of wit and self-mocking can go a long way to making the medicine go down (as I have attempted to do in this book).

As previously noted, *I believe that there are no better teachers for teachers than outstanding, master teachers.* Unfortunately, many times the most common component in schools is the sharing of the same coffee pot in the faculty room. We park in the same lot and walk through the same main office and many times, on spirit day or dress-down Fridays, we wear the same school insignia or logo on the same colored shirt as everyone else in the school. But in how many schools does the sharing, the camaraderie involved in growing professionally, stop there?

When and where are best practices shared by the staff and, more importantly, what can *you do* to provide time and sustenance for that sharing? How do you develop a culture in your school that supports sharing amongst teachers? Are there teachers within your school who can admit to not knowing all there is to know about teaching? Can someone stand up at a meeting and with comfort and candor talk about a time that a lesson or activity went over like a concrete balloon?

Establishing a school culture where people can work together and, more importantly, learn from one another is important. How does a principal allow for the development of collegiality where we learn from each other and are even willing to admit mistakes? That part matters because we all know that many times we learn more from our mistakes than from anything else.

When you are principal and you have already established your open dialogue about best practices through on going grade level or department meetings (a lot smaller than the entire faculty) for a change you might suggest a *Donut and I Once Spilled My Coffee* meeting.

You supply the coffee and donuts (food being the universal language and a comfort zone of all teachers) and they bring with them a lesson that didn't not go well (metaphorically, a time they *spilled the coffee*). Also ask them to reflect on why they thought that and what they plan to try next time to make the lesson more effective. The meeting can develop into some really good laughs and can also produce some excellent exchanges of concepts, ideas, and best practice. You may just find in a year or so, teachers walking into the faculty room (of course, you will not be there) and saying, "Golly, I really spilled the coffee today" and someone responding with, "*Well, tells us about it.*"

It is extremely important that teachers in today's schools have enough pride in what they do and genuinely care about their students and strive to seek professional growth and improvement on their own accord. Being an effective leader is about enabling relationships within the school that provides a comfort zone for that to occur.

Curriculum Development

As the curriculum leader in your school, you must be concerned with *what* is in the curriculum – the content – and *how* to present this as quality learning experiences. You should ask a series of fundamental questions regarding curriculum development such as whether it should have a point of view, is it for social improvement, how do we allow for student cultural differences, and/or how should it be standardized and organized? All great questions whose absence will cause a grease spot [**Grease Spot #34**].

Principals must understand and deal with many curriculum–based educational issues. This revolves around what should be included in the curriculum (content and subject matter) and how it should be presented. Planning curriculum means knowing,

1. The specific facts, skills, and ideas that students need to learn.

2. Staying as up–to–date with technology as needed (or desirable) and learning new knowledge.

3. The breadth and depth (scope) of the subject.

4. How to differentiate in instruction.

5. How all content should be interdependent.

[handwritten margin note: To know when planning curriculum]

A principal must focus on teaching and learning styles so all students have a chance to learn what they are capable of. Content should be constructed to be as relevant as possible for the students, both in and out of school. An important factor, in any economic climate, is how to teach all that is required and with the available time, personnel, and resources.

The key for the school leader is to incorporate the knowledge and ideas from those closest to the curriculum and the students to get to know what the needs and issues are. The more information people have, the better they can do their job. Once again, motivating, inspiring, communicating and leading are at the core of your responsibility.

Documentation

I can think of very little that is more disturbing to me, as I sit in my office at the end of a long day after the last bus has left, then to *have to* chronicle certain events of the day as if I were surreptitiously creating tomes of damaging information to use against others. However, to highlight its importance, I did make the extra key strokes to italicize and underline the words *have to* (there, I did it again). Documentation must *really* be important - and it is [**Grease**

Spot #35]. Your memory of certain issues will not be adequate to chronicle certain unpleasant events that might become necessary to remember during your tenure as principal.

Just prior to the start of each school year, purchase a permanently bound notebook, I use the traditional black and white marble-specked notebook just like the kids (except, I purchase a green or red colored one). It is my most solemn hope that you will only require one and that there will be dozens of pages that have not been written upon. Place the school year on the front and tuck the notebook away where no one knows its location. Sounds covert doesn't it! That book and your appointment calendar will be your *best friends* should you need to attempt to *prove* something. What do I mean by *something*? I am glad you asked.

In my little marble-specked notebook, I record various things that I want to remember. For instance, Mrs. Jones arrived at school ten minutes late today. I record the date and the time she arrived, as well as the time I spoke with her about her lateness. I also make note that I spoke to her about the importance of the timeliness of her arrival and her requirement, by contract, to be on time to school. Now, lest you think I am an Ogre, this would have been Mrs. Jones' second lateness that I observed. Did Mrs. Jones call and indicate she would be late? No. Did I place a written notation in her permanent file for this (archived as her first) lateness (remember, it is her second that you have seen)? No.

However, two weeks later, Mrs. Jones is late to school again! Quick, you know she has been late twice before based upon your observations, but what date was that second time – the first time you spoke with her and what did you say to her at that time? Get the picture because this time, not only am I meeting with Mrs. Jones and talking with her (this is where your appointment calendar comes into play), but I am sending her a little *written* reminder about the requirement for punctuality that will be placed into her personnel file.

Documentation-wise, you have documented only one conversation with her (and even though it is noted in your notebook, she can claim it never occurred), but you now will have a note in your calendar: 10.22.11, Mtg w/Jones; re: 2nd lateness. In the letter to Mrs. Jones, you can note the day and time you spoke with her as well as listing the dates and times of all of her other tardiness as well as your concern for the safety of the students in her classroom because she was not there.

In that letter you also note that she is contractually obligated (if your teacher's contract so states) to be in school at a certain time. It is your expectation that she arrives to school on time. In a situation where her tardiness has meant that students were unsupervised even for a minute, you should note the seriousness of leaving students unsupervised. Note your expectation for her timely arrival at school. At the conclusion of the letter add the following:

I _____ have read and understand all of the above.
(Teacher's Signature)

_____
(Date of Signature)

If this sounds overly tough to you for someone who might be just a few minutes late and might even have a valid reason for being late, please allow me to point something out to you. If a child is hurt in the classroom and the teacher is not there as per contract, the lawsuit filed by the parents for damages will turn your school into a CVS. Now imagine yourself on the witness stand during the lawsuit and the child's attorney asks you how often the teacher has been late. You indicate a couple of times.

"What did you do about it, Dr. Sternberg?"

"Well, I know she has a sick mother who she cares for and early morning can be difficult for her," I say.

"So, you were aware of her tardiness and you did nothing about it and because of that Bob Jones (who hit his head on the corner of a desk while no teacher was in the room and this would not have occurred had he had adequate supervision) has been hospitalized due to your negligence and the negligence of *your* teacher!"

Do you see where this is heading - *I hope so*. Do not be a nice guy/gal. It is just as easily *your future* on the line as well.

Chapter 5

Born or Made: The Genealogy Component Greased at Your Own Risk

Let's wax philosophical for the *briefest* of moments for that is all I can sustain, and only *briefly* because I have always found that practical is better than philosophical. Question, *do you believe that outstanding teachers are born or are they made?* I come down very squarely on this topic and focus my hiring by leaning in the *born* direction. How many times have you read about a famous singer or musician and as you learned more about him or her you discovered that their mom or dad was a musician or singer. This singer's or musician's *roots* were embedded in their genealogic infused gene-pool soul. Their very fiber, their heredity, every corpuscle in their body was grown with this genealogical musical foundation.

I apply the same to teachers. Is it not uncommon to see signs on a building, *Smith and Sons Plumbing* or *Mancuso, Mancuso & Mancuso, Attorneys at Law.* All indicate to me that there is a certain level of proficiency, expertise, a natural ability to teach that is more prevalent and inherent in some people than others. Is this always the case? No. But it is there, I have seen it and been blessed by it, and you should look for it. In the interest of full disclosure, neither of my parents were teachers.

Teaching, working with others engaged in the act of teaching, is a natural calling. You can be taught and trained the basics and you can spew forth what you have learned but in many, many (dare I say most) successful classrooms, I see that natural teaching comes from someone with the ability in their blood. *Great teachers are born and they are limited in number, so get out there and find them fast and before someone else.*

I generally don't like to see resumes that list a person's undergraduate degree in a field not related to education and a graduate degree in education. He or she has tried the business world and now is coming into teaching after finding little or no success (or possibly happiness) outside of teaching. Universities and colleges will award a degree to anyone who finishes their course of study. States issue a teaching license to anyone who finishes a teaching program or a somewhat abbreviated one in a master's program as I have previously pointed out.

I look for applicants who sought out teaching from their first day in college. Is this unfair? Yes, I guess so. But this is my road they are driving down and there are plenty of others who feel differently, so I am not shutting off the entire market to those that do not meet my criteria; it is just my criteria for the school where I am principal. Which candidate spent summers volunteering at camps and/or worked at them? I look for candidates who coached a sport, taught nursery school, or were teaching assistants. I look for someone with teaching in their blood that sees teaching as a passion.

I knew of a very knowledgeable high school physics teacher who knew a heck of a lot about the concepts and laws of physics but could not teach a lick. Picture, if you will, twenty-five marbles dropped at one time on a cement floor that you need to maintain together and you will have an idea of what teaching kindergarten is like. *You may have an idea of how to but can you?* Can you present a subject as complex as Physics to a degree that it is understandable to high school students? Can you create a well-managed classroom full of five-year-olds?

Teaching as easy as riding a bike? Guiding a teacher, either a new one or a veteran teacher, in many ways is like teaching your child how to ride a bicycle. You place your child on the bike and support him or her as you run alongside. As they teeter on the brink of losing their balance and falling, you lend a hand of stability, then let go again and maintain a pace alongside him or her. There comes a time, however, when you let go and they go a distance without you - and eventually, you even let them go around the block without you.

As a principal, should your responsibility come down to teaching teachers how to teach? Just how long are you required, both ethically and morally, to hold onto that bicycle? The college or university has indicated that the perspective teacher has passed all of the required courses and has acquired the basic philosophical knowledge of teaching. The state in which that institution of high education is located has, therefore, granted a probationary license to this person, *based upon their satisfactory completion of the courses required.* The key word here from the state and one lost on many people is the word *probationary.*

Hiring

The high-wire becomes increasingly unencumbered (greaseless, if you will), taut and rigid leading to the platform called retirement when you spend an *inordinate amount of time* making sure you hire the best *of the best.* It goes without saying that this process is also a commitment to your students, teachers, and community to help ensure quality pedagogical practices within the school. However, you will have a major greasy mass dripping from your high-wire as a result of poor hiring practices.

There isn't anything that will have more of an impact on you and the culture of the school than the men and women who you put in the classrooms, behind secretaries' desks, and on the custodial crews. Your high-wire can be greased [**Grease Spot #36**] based upon a less-than-focused hiring agenda and practice, which doesn't serve to cull out the best-of-the-best who show up at your school door as candidates for vacancies. Whom you hire will have *the most significant impact* on the ethos of the building, second only to *you* being hired. Both professionally and personally, the process will ultimately influence the amount and degree of satisfaction and enjoyment that you will take from the school. Parents, kids, superintendents, and board of education members all come and go, but those you hired and the teachers who are granted tenure create a family that might always be around, because once tenured, you cannot easily get rid of anyone. What you are looking to avoid is creating the Addams' Family in your school (feel free to hum and snap your fingers).

The practice of hiring is straightforward, remarkably simple, and logical, and yet the complexity lies in the details. There are no short cuts and due diligence must be paid to the process. During the process, you could be spending a relatively short period of time with someone and, subsequently, making an extremely important decision about that person. You are assessing that person's ability to teach and this person's mores and values in a very short period of time unless you elongate the process. Remember, these people are not going to go on an assembly line to place tires on new Chevys. You are hiring people to help educate the most precious possession that a parent has - his or her child. You are building your faculty family, one person (grain of sand) at a time.

Now the scary part! Think about the *isolation factor* that the process of education supports. The elementary teacher and twenty-five or so kids are basically in a room alone for the vast majority of the time. They shut the door behind them and we leave them alone for a large portion of the day and for hundreds of hours each year. Secondary teachers are with students for usually forty-plus minute periods. Who have you hired, and how good are they? Given the amount of time they will be alone with the students, they had better be darned good! So how are you going to ensure this?

What can you do to get the best possible results and keep your high-wire clean for years to come? The process should begin long before the first advertisement hits the newspaper or is posted on your website. It is important to first understand what you are looking for in the teacher for the particular vacancy.

What special skills might be needed?

What degree of experience might be the best?

What strengths and/or experience would appear to be specifically required?

When you have an idea of what you are looking for, you can place an advertisement that will attract applicants that most closely meet your needs. At the same time, you need to start developing an interview that will highlight potential strengths of the candidates as well as bringing to the surface any areas of concern.

What do you look for in a resume?

How do you select the candidates that you want to interview?

What university preparation makes a candidate appear to have strong potential?

What work experience have they had in the field or related experience?

In addition, look on the resume for a significant amount of time spent as a volunteer or compensated work with young people at camps, tutoring, volunteer work, etc. If possible, having more than one person reviewing resumes is a good idea. List your priorities and qualifications for the specific position that you would like the candidate to have. But don't get so locked in that you miss someone just outside the parameters of your priority list. And do not be afraid to hire someone new to the field. Because someone has graduated in May and wants to teach in your school starting in September should not eliminate them. I have hired first year teachers who can teach rings around some fifteen year veterans.

The hiring process should, at the minimum, entail:

- Determining what you need to fill a vacancy.
- Advertisement of the vacancy with as many specifics about the job as possible.
- Personal contacts with colleagues/colleges/universities in an effort to find qualified candidates.
- Resume screening.
- Creating a set of interview questions that focuses in on the qualifications that you are seeking.
- Screening interviews.
- Demonstration lessons.

- Teacher interview committee.
- Reference checks.
- Checking Facebook pages* of your final three candidates.
- Google* the name of your final three candidates.

* Got nothing better to do on a Tuesday evening? Jump onto Facebook and Google and run the names of your final two or three candidates that you have for positions within your school. Why? Well, you'll know the answer to that question based upon what you find or do not find.

As you develop a cohort of educators in your building, you want to make sure that you diversify your staff in as many ways as possible. Be careful not to load your faculty with educators from the same *local* area universities or colleges. Be careful not to have everyone looking the same. If your school does not mirror the society that your kids will have to function in, then you are doing them a huge disservice. Seemingly contradictory to the above paragraph, don't be afraid to target universities and/or colleges that you have already culled successful candidates from and send a letter to the placement office of those schools requesting recommendations of candidates.

You are looking for someone with passion, enthusiasm, skill, sensitivity, knowledge, heart, humor and a *natural ability* to teach. You want someone who takes to a classroom filled with kids as easily and naturally as a fish swims. I am not willing to debate whether great teachers are born or great teachers are made. This is my book, my experiences, my theory (and if you don't like that, stop reading and please go out and write your own book and please send me a copy) because I truly believe that either you are *born to teach* or you are not. You cannot *make* an outstanding teacher; they are born, and I want to find those people. Don't believe me and don't want to search for those *natural teachers*? Good, then more will be left out there for me - and good luck to you, my friend!

Trick Question

Also be cognizant of the fact that you are ultimately looking for the best teacher, not the person who interviews the best. By making the interview process just that, a process, you help to protect yourself. You wouldn't marry someone after just one date, would you? O.K., maybe *you* would, but it would have to have been quite a date! However, statistically, let me advise you that is probably not a good idea.

Be careful of those teachers who appear to be a *Kid-Magnet*. This may sound like the antithesis of what you are trying to accomplish; however, you are looking for someone who is respected for his or her ability to reach students on a level where the students know that this person is there to assist and guide them through their lessons and activities. The kids do not need and, I submit, are not looking for a friend and you shouldn't be either. Kid-Magnets are best hired for summer camps, not necessarily in your school.

I want a resume that is clean, professional looking, error-free (unlike this book) that has no employment gaps. The cover letter needs to specifically note the job the candidate is looking for and two or three sentences about what related experiences make them a *perfect fit* for the vacancy. I do not want a mass-produced letter and *never* will I read beyond, To Whom It May Concern. I want someone who is putting in the effort to create a letter/resume *just* for this job. If you are not showing me some *significant effort to get the job*, what I can I expect when you have the job?

Never establish a limit on the number of screening interviews that you will conduct to find candidates to move onto the next round. The bottom line concept for me has always been, *how many frogs will I need to kiss to find a prince or princess?* The answer is a simple, as many as necessary. Please send me Phisohex.

Day in and day out you have high expectations for the faculty to establish the educational health of the school, and now it is time for *you* to produce. One of your credibility issues, as you are viewed by others, will be vested in whom you hire. The quality of the colleague that you place into the existing faculty will go a long way to establishing you as a serious and credible leader. You will be measured by that yardstick! It is my *absolute* belief that the best educators in the school want nothing but the very best colleague in that classroom next to them - and the best secretaries, the best custodians and yes, the best principal!

In our field, most times it is an accurate statement that a candidate will accept just about any job that they are offered because there are so few jobs available. This then leads one to a point that might seem useless given that statement. However, one foundational premise that drives me is how I want to be viewed by the candidate. I assume a role that makes the candidate feel like a welcomed guest in my house during the entire hiring process. When they leave the interview, I want them to want this job based upon a number of reasons, not the least of which is how professionally and warmly they were treated.

Screening Interviews

I dedicate approximately forty minutes for each screening interview. I suggest standardizing your questions and format so that you can compare responses - apples to apples, oranges to oranges. However, don't be so structured that a *natural* conversation cannot breakout during the interview. After a few years of experience, you will come to realize that if those standardized questions during an interview start to turn into a *dialogue/conversation* between you and the candidate about pedagogy; that is a very good first signal. Don't be afraid to deviate from the script of questions if a response from the candidate is interesting and starts to lead in an interesting direction – whether positive and negative. Some interviews can last longer than forty minutes (and that is a very good sign), and there are some that just need a mercy killing and should have been stopped long before. During an interview, if you start hearing the opening to the television show *60 Minutes* in your head, that also is not a good sign.

I begin the interview with a sincere warm welcome and brief overview of what the available position is:

Good morning (afternoon) Mr./Ms./Mrs./Dr._____, welcome to the _____ School. Thank you for your interest in our school and for making yourself available for this interview. As you are aware, we have a vacancy in our school/department (specify the grade level and/or department). I have reviewed your resume and was very impressed with your general background, education, and experiences.

I have a series of questions that I would like you to respond to, questions that I will be asking all of the candidates for this position. At the end of this screening interview, I will ask if you have any questions about the position and will provide you with information about the next step in the hiring process. I will also afford you an opportunity to present any closing statement that you would like to make and/or present any points about yourself or your experiences that will serve to enhance your candidacy that maybe my questions did not bring out.

Prior to starting with my questions, I would ask that you begin by presenting pertinent components of your resume, live and in person.

I sit back and listen and try to imagine a few different things. For instance:

If I were a student in this teacher's class, would I feel comfortable?

Would I think that this teacher would be fair and yet academically demanding?

Does this candidate exude confidence?

I also think about if I were a parent of a child in this person's class.

How would I react to him or her?

Would I get a sense that this teacher cares about my child?

Would I be comforted knowing that he or she is my child's teacher?

Do I feel that my child's teacher is knowledgeable in curricula and is warmly professional?

As a colleague, is this person someone I could professionally get along with as a member of the school team? I listen for what they say *and* what they don't say. Following the question-and-answer period:

Thank you (Candidate's name) for your responses. Do you have any questions about the position, the school and/or the school district that will assist you in making a decision about this vacancy?

Following that:

(Candidate's name) is there anything that you would like to let me know about yourself that maybe my questioning did not bring out or any statement that you might like to make that would serve to enhance your candidacy?

Following this, the candidates usually are interested in the next step(s) and a time table for the decision making process. You should divulge as much as you are comfortable with, but you should not be so specific as to lock yourself into specific weeks for the next step. Let the candidate know you will keep them informed.

I will keep you informed of your progress in the process, and I would appreciate your letting me know if your status should change, so that I can adjust accordingly. Thank you for presenting yourself. It was a pleasure meeting you.

During the interview, I throw in a question or two that comes from left field just to see how the candidate thinks on their feet. For example, *"If you were a car, what kind would you be and why?" "If you could have dinner with three people from the past, living or deceased, who would they be and why?"* Some of my colleagues hate asking these questions, but I love them, and it is just one more layer of information about how candidates would potentially handle a fastball, high and in tight.

(www.SchoolHireRight.com has a program that makes comparing candidate strengths and creates a process that standardizes the questioning, responses, and the reporting of interviews. It is a product that serves to standardize and allows fair candidate comparisons.)

DEMO

I interview approximately eight to eleven candidates for *every* vacancy (or more if necessary). *Your perseverance will be rewarded!* Following the screening interviews, a demonstration lesson (*demo* lesson) is imperative. I do not have a ballpark number of demos per vacancy. The bottom line is if during the interview I sense that I would like to see a candidate in front of a class, then they *get demo'd*.

Remember, you want to hire the best teacher, not the person that interviews the best, and those two elements are obviously not directly related. Many times, the person who interviews the best may not be the best teacher. Conversely, I have two teachers presently in the school, each of whom gave a *very* weak interview. They were extremely nervous. However, something came through in those interviews that sparked my interest in seeing each in a classroom. They each shined during the *demo*, and their *natural teaching talents and skills* were evident during the *demo* lesson. They are currently two of the best teachers in the school. Some people can talk a good educational philosophy and practice yet it is quite the opposite to put that philosophy into effective practice. *Your job will be to tell the difference!*

A little tip - I am constantly amazed at the vast majority of candidates who come to an interview carrying their portfolio. They sit with that puppy in front of them, or to their side, or against their chair, and only at the end of the interview, they inquire about whether or not I would like to see their portfolio. I always say *no*, politely, but no thank you. For me, at that time in the interview, it is after the fact! Think about this. <u>They brought a teaching tool with them to help you learn more about them and they didn't use the teaching tool they brought with them</u>! I have had a few candidates *use* the portfolio as a teaching tool *during* the interview. They had an in-depth knowledge of their portfolio and it was more than a *scrapbook*. As they were responding to a question, they used the portfolio to support or illustrate their statement (remember to think *natural teacher*). Think how great it is when that happens and the candidate opens the portfolio and turns it towards you and uses it as if he or she was teaching you! If a candidate does this, I have three words and ten exclamation marks for you - *DEMO* **THIS PERSON!!!!!!!!!!**

I cannot overemphasize or over value the demonstration lesson as an integral part of the interview process. This is a brief thirty to forty minute lesson with a fixed academic focus. I request an outline of the lesson and let the candidate know the specific topic I want them to teach, the number of students in the class, their general academic ability range and grade level, and anything else in particular I think is relevant to the class. I always ask the classroom teacher to stay and observe the candidate as well.

Yes, the *demo* is contrived, limited, and somewhat plastic. However, where or how else will you be able to see how the candidate performs in front of a room filled with students? Set up the *demo* lesson by selecting the appropriate field or grade level. Obviously this will depend on where your vacancy is. After getting the support from the regular classroom teacher, inform the students in the class the day before of what will be happening. On the day of the *demo* lesson, provide all students a nametag with their first names on them.

What should you look for in a demonstration lesson? I am always less concerned with the actual lesson than I am with the interaction between the candidate and the students. When I have some degree of comfort with the way the candidate is handling him/herself with the students, I then can turn my attention to the lesson itself. A natural teacher (have I mentioned my bias here) will be just that, natural but in charge with a sense of command, comfortable and yet directed, self-assured, confident, and having a sense of authority without demanding it. Also observe how the students react to him or her!

Teacher Interview Committee

Following a successful demonstration lesson, selected candidates are sent to the teacher interview committee. The teacher interview committee is a great opportunity to see and listen to a candidate once again prior to making a final recommendation to your superintendent. Teachers run the interview and ask their own questions. I am the facilitator introducing the candidate to the committee members and starting and concluding the interview with a brief statement very similar to one I noted previously. This will provide you with a chance to observe and to listen! It also obviously provides an opportunity to give teachers leadership roles, which is the reason I ask them to serve on the interview committee.

Many times, teachers will be very, very emphatic about who they want working with them. Just watch out for the *Halo Effect* as well as the *Intimidation Factor*. You do not want someone hired just because they look good or seem sweet and kind. Remember Kid-Magnet? It applies here. Some teachers fresh out of school with new ideas and enthusiasm may intimidate some veteran faculty members sitting on the committee. Be cognizant of the *limits* of the committee as well as their potential strengths.

Teachers complete the same rating sheet (SchoolHireRight) that I use, and all sheets will eventually be forwarded to the central office. At the conclusion of the round of teacher interviews, I meet with the committee. After everyone has completed their rating sheets, we analyze and discuss each candidate. I break the discussion into two components. One is the general pros and cons for each candidate. Each committee member takes a turn noting any positive comments and/or any concerns that they have about the candidate. We do this for each candidate. The second is to rank order of the candidates. The essential question I ask of the group for each candidate is simply, *"Would you want to work with this person? Why or why not?* Now, here is the rub. How much do the ratings of the teachers on the committee count? We have discussed, at length, shared decision-making, and the key words here are *shared* and *decision-making*. The decision and question for you is *how much sharing can you afford to allow in this particular decision?*

The System is Working Just Fine

The proof of the pudding is in the tasting.........

As part of mentoring, I assigned a veteran teacher to a new teacher who was serving as a leave replacement for the school year for a teacher in that mentor's grade. The veteran teacher whom I have a great deal of confidence in is an outstanding teacher who worked with the new teacher throughout the year. There were indications that the new teacher had some significant instructional gaps, and the mentor teacher was working with her on a regular basis supported by others within the building, including me.

As the year ended there was a full-time, probationary position available in our school. Leave replacement teachers still have to go through the regular and full hiring process, and this leave replacement teacher applied and went through the process. She was passed on all the way to the teacher interview committee round. As circumstances came to be, her mentor for the year happened to be on the committee. After the interviews were concluded, we began to discuss the candidates.

And here, my friends, is where you know your *system* is working. With her eyes welled up with tears, the mentor spoke of how hard the leave replacement had tried and how sweet and nice she was and how all the kids loved her. However, after working with her and realizing all that was done for her, the mentor said the applicant still lacked the basic knowledge and performance level skills of even a new teacher and said she was not the strongest candidate we had interviewed. *We did not hire her.*

This told me a great deal about our *system*. One, that this teacher wanted *only the best* working with her. Second, that even trying as hard as she could, the mentor saw significant flaws in the leave replacement teacher's knowledge and teaching skills. Most important, at least to me, was that the mentor never thought for a moment that I would think she was any less a teacher or a mentor because she could not make this weak teacher into an effective teacher. It always comes back to *trust* between the teacher and principal, doesn't it.

....................and the pudding tastes sweet!

Bottom Line

You might encounter some extremely strong teachers who express a quid-pro-quo attitude in terms of their dedicating time and effort to the teacher interview committee. Some teachers want to be able to have a thumbs-up or thumbs-down finality of input for each candidate. There will be some, on the other extreme, who want *you* to make the decision. You want to lean toward the latter. I have opted for a simple discussion at the beginning of the process in which I talk with the committee about their role. I tell them the committee is *advisory*. I want them to ask whatever questions they want (and part of this discussion is a review of the types of questions that are illegal to ask), and that their rating sheets will be seen by the superintendent. I believe this tells people with the strong opinions that their voices will be heard and considered.

However, given my extended interactions with the candidates (a previous interview, a demo lesson, watching the teacher interview committee interview, and possible reference contacts); I take their input into account *weighed* with all of the information that I have. I also make them aware that they, along with me, are *just* components in the process. Reference checks made by the superintendent can negate even our strongest opinions. These reference checks are always confidential.

So who sits on this committee? You might find yourself in a situation that, by contract, teachers are selected by a certain process (usually union appointment) and sit on the committee, or you may the luxury of selecting your own committee. Certainly, your hands are tied with the former but if you are allowed to select, make sure you select people whose opinions you trust. Now, doesn't that seem obvious? Rule of thumb: Select people you admire in the classroom. I will continue not to accept requests to sit on the committee. I also shy away from letting people assist in selecting their own replacement. There are a whole mess of reasons for not heading down that road, not the least of which is that your requirements for the position may sound like you think the retiree lacked those qualities, and you are looking for someone better. The emotion of putting in one's retirement papers and eventually realizing their days in school are numbered is difficult enough without this added anxiety.

With each outstanding teacher you add to the faculty cohort, an additional grain of sand is added to the beach (you remember, we were at this beach with Ben and Jerry) and your high-wire is clean and clear. Each positive action by your newly hired teacher adds yet another grain of sand to your beach and maintains a grease-free high-wire. However, be forewarned, each less-than-spectacular teacher added to or kept on your staff *takes a shovel full* of sand away. General observation: Sand is added a grain at a time, and most times it is removed by the shovel full.

The Greasy New Teacher

The expectation of *every* parent who has a student in the class of a teacher who is new to teaching is that this will be an *outstanding* school year for their child. However, most do not want a teacher with limited experience. That defines every brand-new, fresh-out-of-the-box teacher. I have hired teachers so new, so fresh-out-of-the-box, that when they came into school the first day, they still had some of those Styrofoam packing peanuts statically clung to them. The expectation of all parents is getting the teacher with experience; otherwise, can you *guarantee* the new teacher is as good as the veteran teacher? [**Grease Spot #37**]

This really sums up the *sorry state* of our profession. We put brand new, fresh out of the box (packing Styrofoam still clinging), into a classroom by themselves and say, *"Go!"* Isn't it the expectation of parents that the teacher spending his/her first day, week, month, or year in a classroom will have the same expertise as a teacher who has been doing the job for ten years? No? Well, ask any parent what they expect! Children get only *one shot* at first grade, fourth grade, eighth grade science, earth science, or AP English. The parental expectation is that the new teacher is as good as, if not better than, the veteran. And where are you in the mix? How do you get a first-year teacher up to speed - and quickly (again, think natural born teacher)?

The next time you or your child needs surgery, consider seeking out a surgeon who just graduated from medical school and moved into an established practice of board certified, experienced surgeons. On the very first day in the practice, is this new member of the practice going to do the surgery alone? Does this new surgeon walk into the operating room, close the door behind him or her, and start? Do I have any volunteers to be their first victim, I mean patient?

Does the new attorney, fresh out of law school, walk directly into a courtroom and argue a case? Do they walk into the courtroom, close the door behind them and start? (P.S. This *new* attorney is handling your lawsuit against the *new* surgeon who botched your hip replacement surgery.) How about the engineer working on his first day at a nuclear power plant?

So why do we take a new teacher, fresh out of a school of education and allow that person to walk into a classroom, alone with twenty-five students, close the door behind them, and ask them to start to teach in a *spectacular* fashion. No need to email me the answers to these questions. I think I have a handle on the answers, *unfortunately*.

Just Too New

The years that a doctor or attorney (or a plumber or an electrician or a car mechanic or nuclear engineer, you get the picture) practice under the direct supervision of a veteran is significant. These people *apprentice* alongside someone with more experience and knowledge so they can learn their craft. This has always been one of my deepest concerns, and I could never understand why principals have never taken a stronger stance on attempting to force colleges and universities to develop an intern approach to training teachers and why the states have not *required*, prior to certifying teachers and granting a license, a two to three year, *paid* internship. I know why, and so do you. The one-word answer starts with M and ends with Y and has ONE in the middle. And, if you suggest that student teaching is that apprenticeship or some form of teacher mentor program, I suggest you close this book, try to get your money back from where you purchased it, and use that money to purchase the latest John Grisham novel because, obviously, fiction is your true love.

New teachers (as do doctors, lawyers, mechanics, HVAC technicians, chefs, etc.), require years to develop skills, and yet teachers are thrown into classrooms on their first day with the expectation that they will perform as well as a veteran teacher. Parents demand this, and you as principal pray for it. One former superintendent of mine had the philosophy that the college/university had granted a degree to the person, indicating their competency, and the state had issued a certification/license; therefore, it is not the district's responsibility to teach this person how to teach. The state and the college/university indicate the graduate knows how to teach. Where do you, as a principal, draw the line and what degrees of assistance do you and can you offer the new teacher? What comments do you make to the parent who questions the new teacher's skill, content knowledge, and ability? My former superintendent's position was simply, if they can teach keep them, if not, fire them! His point was that it is not our responsibility to teach them how to teach. I concur only because of the system we are stuck with, but I contend there is better way, and a paid, three-year apprenticeship is that way.

How can I concur? As altruistic and philanthropic as you would like to see yourself, the bottom line is *time*. You will not have enough of it (time) to teach someone to teach. Guide? Yes. Mentor? Yes. Remember the bicycle analogy? A guide-on-the-side who will continually run alongside someone, day-in, day-out is unrealistic. You decide when and where, in your mind, you want to let go. How many times are you willing to reach out to grab the bicycle seat to steady the teacher? How many times are you willing to pick them up after they have fallen and let them start again. It really is that simple.

You are not going to have time to daily hold the hand of the teacher. Did I say teacher? No. Teachers! Consider that you could have a few new teachers each year and as many as eight to ten, all within their first three years of teaching. How thin can you spread yourself? The observation and evaluation system allows you to guide that teacher on his or her bike for a limited number of times, and it is spread as thin as butter on warm toast, especially when you factor in all of your other responsibilities. Now, *please* go back and read my thoughts on a naturally born teacher who takes to the classroom like a fish to water. *No need to email me your apologies; it is the thought that counts.*

Time Deficiency

You will start to become a little hardened. You will become a little less philanthropic with your time because your time will be divided in many ways, by many people, and you can only pedal (I will continue with the bike metaphor) so fast. It will be very easy at this point in time to have people (teachers) slip past you. They become tenured, and you are married to them – until death (or retirement) do you part – *if you are not careful*. This is where you need to spend the vast majority of your time. Investing time to monitor and continually evaluating new staff. Do not forget about them by accident or on purpose. Make mental and physical notes to yourself to get your butt into the classroom of all your new teachers *regularly*. Let me spell out regularly - I spell it, A-T L-E-A-S-T O-N-C-E E-V-E-R-Y T-H-R-E-E D-A-Y-S during their first year, and if you are comfortable with their performance, once or twice every week during the second year. This is above and beyond the formal observations that you will be making according to contract and/or district policy. At this stage, the parents of the kids in the class of the new teacher should not know them better than you do! If you do not have time to do this, then you are not spending your time wisely. And, if you delegate this responsibility to anyone else (assistant principal, department chair, area director, etc.), with all due respect, you are being foolish and not doing your job.

Until your state changes processes of certifying and licensing teachers and establishes a long-term internship/apprenticeship, guess who is their *long-term* internship mentor. *That would be you!* You are going to have to establish in your mind:

What is outstanding teaching?

What does it look like?

What does it sound like? What does it feel like? What does it smell and taste like?

What minimum level of performance will you accept from a first-year teacher, a second-year teacher, and are these people on a track to become an *outstanding* teacher?

It is your high-wire; you can make efforts to keep it grease-free, or you can potentially have it well-greased based upon what you do. You start setting your foot down on the slippery wire when you are not clear in your mind where that line of acceptability and excellence is and you have not established in your mind a determination not to cross that line in the sand.

How much of a person's ability or raw talent is workable, trainable, and (this is going to sound really bad but), how much time are you able to *realistically* spend and dedicate to this person? How much *available time* is there to teach what someone does not know, factoring in how much training might be necessary? Hire a poor-performing teacher and you find yourself defending that teacher for the remainder of his/her career (or your career) – a slippery high-wire at best! Also, realistically, do you have the time to take a poor-performing neophyte and turn him or her into a great teacher? To what degree should the colleges, universities and state licensing bureaus have to *ensure* that *highly competent* people are graduating and are being licensed? Is your job as principal to take anyone who comes along with a degree and a license and turn that frog into a prince or princess?

When I go shopping for peaches, I just don't take what is offered; I select as I look through the pile, much the same as I would select only promising teacher candidates from the applicant pool. After selecting, I make a judgment if I want to keep the peach or after working with the teacher for a year or two (at the most), making a determination about continuation of employment. Select the Mackinaws, Jerry!

To Be or Not To Be, Tenured

One of the most ridiculous aspects of our profession is, forgive me, tenure. I am aware of all the laws and historical background surrounding tenure and the reasons tenure became law in many states. Notwithstanding, how can a principal function successfully when the immediate world around him/her is tenured? How can a principal ensure the continuation of excellence when the immediate world around him/her has tenure? The answer to both those questions is the same - *not easily and it is darn near impossible*. Now, please go back and review the section on hiring (and natural born teachers).

As you enter a new building, there will obviously be tenured staff members. As you witness their classroom skills and learn how effective they are you are kind of stuck with having what you have. Those teachers who are found lacking will be dealt with in a manner that we will discuss later. When I see those teachers who are lacking skills, I promise myself that the principal who will take my place will never utter the words, *"Who gave this teacher tenure?"*

Now, if you are of the mindset that your high-wire is always greased by others, and you have no choice but to deal with it that can be accurate. However, there are times and places where you can control the grease and even whether or not there is grease at all. Hiring highly quality staff members, as we have discussed, is one way of avoiding placing grease on your own high-wire. A subset of hiring is the performance of those teachers you hired and your ability to improve their instructional capabilities or to let them go before you become *married to them for life* through granting them tenure.

Tenure should not be a goal or an end that people seek, and it should never be conveyed that way to your non-tenured teachers. Rather, to me it signifies a beginning, and that message must be conveyed to your teachers because it does not occur naturally in our environment. New teachers view tenure as a goal and that is wrong. It is your responsibility to make sure that the first day a teacher joins your staff and every day after that, including the first day after they earn tenure, is one filled with self-reflection and growth. Your expectation of your teachers has a direct and lasting influence on the expectation of themselves. If they read from your actions or words that tenure is the ultimate goal, then you are sending the wrong message. Tenure is a beginning, not fruition!

During my thirty two years as a principal, I have never denied tenure to anyone. Please reread that last sentence. However, I have denied continuation of probation to nine teachers. Please reread that last sentence. I looked at each one of those denials as *my* failure.

What did I miss during the interview process?

What was said or not said that I missed?

Why was my judgment inaccurate?

I try to remember the interview process that he or she went through to look at what should have signaled to me the poor potential of this teacher. Secondly, and upon reflection, what didn't I do enough of, or what could I have done better to assist these teachers in reaching a plateau of excellence that would have allowed them to continue in the school? The harsh reality is not on them as inferior teachers but on me for (a) not recognizing their lack of potential prior to hiring, or (b) not being able to improve their instructional ability. It is, I suggest the only way you should look at this issue - and this from a man who thinks quality teachers are born, not made.

After each situation of not recommending continuation of probation, I meticulously go through my interview notes and rating sheets (I take notes about a candidate on the back of my rating sheet). I go back to the demonstration rating sheet and my notes for that segment of the process as well. I want this to be a learning experience for me!

I asked myself *when did I first start to have a concern*. Then I asked, *"What did I do about it?*

The questions just cascade from there:
How many conferences (both formal and informal) did I have with the teacher?

What direction/assistance did I provide?

What kinds and how deep was the support provided? What seemed to work and what did not work? Why?

What were the bottom line weaknesses, and were they so significant they could not be successfully addressed and corrected?

Would one more year of support have made a difference?

What would this teacher probably be like five years from now if he/she were allowed to stay here?

These questions and your actions are significant. You are dealing with someone's professional career and a denial of continuation of probation *will*, make no mistake about it, have an impact on their personal life as well. You have to be *absolutely sure* that you gave *every* person the fullest and best opportunity to succeed. You have to look yourself in the mirror each day, and if you did the best you could by the person, then when you put your head on the pillow at night, you can sleep the sleep of the just and righteous based upon your efforts *on their behalf* in school.

Two Years Maximum

I believe and suggest to you that you give teachers new to your building two years to establish themselves and review the blueprint for success you have created for them. The first responsibility is yours. What have you done to ensure success of your new teachers? During those formative days and weeks of their first year in the building, you must be the driving force. You must provide them with the tools for success. This starts with the basics of getting to know and feeling comfortable in the setting (where the bathrooms are) to providing them with the books, curricula outlines and maps, scope and sequence of their particular area of responsibility. Incorporating them into the building by introducing them to and folding them into the ethos and processes of the building by meeting and talking with key staff personnel, teachers of the same grade level or department, other administrators, secretaries, custodial personnel, etc., and providing both formal and informal mentoring.

You should know before tenure decision time whether someone is *a keeper*. If you are starting the thought process of whether or not to grant tenure at the beginning of year three, you have not been thinking about this teacher enough [**Grease Spot #38**]. It is your responsibility to be extremely clear with teachers on probation about your expectations and extremely clear about where he or she is *not* meeting those expectations. It is going to be tough. You will need to be tough. Warm, gentle, sincere, supportive, congenial, professional also, but crystal clear in terms of your expectations and that is where tough comes into the picture. The best thing you can do for a new teacher is to hook that person up with one or two teachers whose performance is outstanding and who you would want this new teacher to emulate. I am extremely clear with new teachers about following the lead of *specific* teachers (I name them) with whom they will be working: watch this person, breathe the way they do, walk the way they do, teach like them, eat like them and, if necessary, learn to teach like them.

If, after all of your best and most sincere efforts, the result is not what is best for kids, then you will have *an easy decision*. The decision will be easy if you have done your part; however, delivering the final message will not be easy. You need to keep your eye on the goal. You want the best for your students and the only way that can be achieved is by having the best teachers. That is a concrete tenet of your job and outside of health and safety issues, it is your chief responsibility. If you can look yourself square in the eye and say you have done everything possible to assist this neophyte, but the results have not been acceptable, then you should be comfortable in your decision and your subsequent action.

Rocks in Pocket

This is will be a less than flattering view of who I am and the degree of seriousness and dedication I apply to the concept of making sure that less than highly competent personnel are *not* hired. After you have expended *all* the energy that you possibly can toward hiring the best educator starting with the due diligence applied during the interview process and expanding into the first weeks, months, and well into the first year of their time in your school, when you have made that final decision that the person is not working out, you must set your sights on their departure strategy.

In the private sector, when an employee is let go, the departure is rather expedient. People are literally here today and gone later that day! In our world, teachers are notified that they will not be asked back sometimes months in advance of the last day of school and now that employee is in your school with kids and knows that he or she will not be coming back next year. Given the short supply of teaching jobs available, this can be a career death sentence. And for the last two months of school and possible their educational career, they are with you.

These people will be seeking every way possible for reconsideration and seeking you to extend a hand to assist them. My strongest suggestion to you is that once you have made up your mind, there is no assistance you can provide - you have done *everything* you can already. These people have driven themselves to the edge of the cliff and are about to fall off. As they reach back to you for that once last shot at redemption, you must not reach out to them - you will appear indecisive and your actions will be misconstrued. What you must do as they are leaning over the cliff is put rocks in their pockets! I am sorry, I know this sounds terrible.

Remember, you are done! You have done *everything* you can to assist this teacher in becoming qualified enough to be asked back for a third probationary year and he or she has not performed. You no longer can be supportive. You can be cordial, professional, nice, but no longer supportive.

You will be asked by the teacher to *write a letter of recommendation* so that they can get a job someplace else. You must be *extremely* careful what you write in that letter, if you write one at all. It is after all a letter of recommendation and you are not recommending him or her to continue in your school, how could you for someplace else? Think about it! How can you write a positive letter about someone you are firing? And if you give that letter to the teacher to attach to his or her resume that is crazy - never do that. When asked I indicate that they should include me on their resume and I will acknowledge that they were employed here and I will support the positive aspects of their time here. That is all I ever say to the teacher. You need to be careful to not set yourself up by writing a positive letter about someone *you're firing*.

The teacher will have to note you on their resume as their last employer and you might get a phone call at some point in the future from a fellow principal about this teacher who is seeking a job in their school. You have libel and slander issues galore here, be careful what you say and write. I use the *pregnant pause* concept when I am asked about someone who worked in my school that I would not recommend. You will always be asked this question, *if given the opportunity would you hire this person back?* When I hear that question, I simply repeat back slowly, *"...would I hire (him or her) back"* followed by a *long* pause - a *pregnant pause* - and then I say, *"all candidates for vacancies in our district are provided with an equal opportunity for whatever vacancy is available."* If pressed one step further, I will comment that the person was *"nice, came to work on time, and was punctual with paperwork and attendance at meetings."* If my colleague does not *get it* at that point in time, maybe they deserve each other.

FYI

Let me please point out that at the first indication that any first year teacher could *potentially* not work out, you *must* start to document your efforts. Certainly, you will have your observations to illustrate areas of concern and weakness. But, you must also maintain *notes to yourself* that indicate EVERYTHING; let me make this point again and a little clearer: E-V-E-R-Y-T-H-I-N-G that you say to and/or have done for this teacher. Note the day, time, and topic of your meetings, and make sure they appear on your professional desk calendar. Note the teachers you sent into the classroom to assist the teacher, and note the times you covered that teacher's class (more about this later), so the teacher could observe another teacher. Note the conferences or workshops you sent the teacher to and/or the suggestions that you made to the teacher about attendance at a conference (at district expense) that he or she did not go to. You are painstakingly chronicling every effort you have made to assist this teacher.

There will come a point in time, if this person is not going to be continued, when he or she will become desperate to maintain his or her job and may become angry about what they perceive is happening *to them*, and they will flail out at anything and anyone they see as causing this - and that, my friend, *will be you*. Lifeguards are taught that as they approach a person who is drowning, to dive under the water and come up behind the drowning person. If you approach from the front, the person in danger will reach out, grasp you with a death-grip, and you will both drown. Take that metaphor and apply it to the situation of a teacher, knowing that they will not be asked back. It is, therefore, critically important to make sure you have documented every effort, suggestion, and when you first noticed *each* concern. Also document the teacher's reaction and rate of growth to each effort - think, RTI for grownups.

1 in a 1,000,000

Picture this improbable situation (and if you think it is improbable, take the hayseed out of your mouth, take your hair out of pigtails, and stop looking under your bed for the tooth fairy). Go back to the life-threatening situation a drowning victim is in and their desperation. The teacher about to not be asked back is asked by the union lawyer (and they will be racing to the union lawyer), *"Has the principal ever suggested you look nice, you were wearing a nice dress, you have lovely hair, that suit and tie look great on you, have you lost weight, etc.?"* Do you see where I am heading? No. O.K., the union lawyer *may* try to paint a picture that you were not fair to the teacher. The teacher was uncomfortable with the principal because he or she felt that the principal was making uncomfortable suggestions or comments. The teacher about to be dismissed did not report them because he or she was afraid of potential consequences or the anger of the principal. Improbable? Incredible? We are talking about someone's *career-life*. Does the union lawyer care if she or he is a good teacher? *No!* The union lawyer wants to win! Your lapses of good *professional* judgment are fodder for a sharp attorney.

I have supplied you with the paints, crayons, and paper; you go on painting this picture. Think drowning victim. Don't ever get yourself into any potential situation(s) by your words and/or deeds, as innocent as they might appear at the outset. Paranoid? No, just be *very* careful. Save the compliments for your wife, husband, life-partner, boyfriend, girlfriend, or significant other, and keep professional situations - *professional*.

If you can show to whomever: the teacher's union representative, the superintendent, the teacher's lawyer, etc. (and you will eventually see all of these people – I was once even approached by the father of one teacher to whom I was denying continuation of probation about why I was *"doing this"* to his daughter) the copious notes of all of your efforts, it will be not only impressive but will demonstrate, by your documentation, your judicious and *fair* (key word here) of the issue. Documentation is your friend. (I did not show my notes to that woman's father.)

Postscript. The teachers' union president is there for one reason and only one reason and there is only one reason they can be involved in a situation like this. They are there to ensure that *due process* has been afforded to their member, period. So, need I mention the importance of documentation again!

The Halo Effect
An Easily Greased and Yet Hard to See Section of the High-Wire

I remember this cute young teacher who, after hiring her, I began to realize after numerous informal and formal observations, things were not going well in her class. The *Halo Effect* had taken over, and her attractiveness, youth, relationship with her students (and their parents) hid from their view some serious pedagogical flaws and inadequacies. After months of working with her and having others work with her, she still was not implementing an effective academic program and/or maintaining a focused academic setting. The kids loved her, but they were learning very little. Midway through her second school year with us, I made the decision to cut bait and did not offer her a job next year. I did not recommend her for continuation of probation. She used the soapbox of the faculty room (you remember the faculty room) to plead her case with her colleagues and worse, she took her case *public*. She approached numerous parents and asked them each to write a letter on her behalf to me and to forward a copy of the letter to the superintendent and the board of education. She claimed that no one assisted her (especially me) and that she did not receive enough observations and direction. I was made out to be a *bully* and the bad guy [**Grease Spot #39**].

Remember when I mentioned about *documentation* and its importance? I had all of my notes, copies of memos, directions, times of meetings, who worked with her and when. Of course, I also had all the dates of my observations *and* had listed in my calendar all the meetings I had with her. I even kept a copy of an early observation of her that I never wrote up because the lesson was so bad. I gave her a second chance and observed her the following week *after* two meetings with her. I documented her up and out the wazoo.

All this information was given to her, her union representative, the superintendent and subsequently, by the superintendent, to our board of education. Yet we were not allowed to publicize any of it, and she kept on bad mouthing me. The students and the parents were caught up in her niceness – the Halo Effect – and could not understand how *I* could not be bringing her back - after all, *everyone loves her.*

D-O-C-U-M-E-N-T-A-T-I-O-N! A lesson I hope you will learn *very* early and will practice extremely well. Write everything down somewhere! Documentation keeps the high-wire from getting *really* greasy. In the eyes of your superintendent and the BOE as well as that of the teachers' union president, I was a force to be reckoned with.

So with this working against you – the Halo Effect – how do you get faculty and staff to see you as a fair leader? First, don't sweat the small stuff. No matter what is said in the faculty room and how many people seem to be in agreement with the aggrieved party, most people:

1. Are not supportive of him or her.
2. Are silently applauding your stance.

While we are on the subject, here is a great opportunity to walk-the-talk. If you profess to wanting and expecting an outstanding faculty, there will be times when less than excellent people may make their way through the hiring process and not be all that you had hoped they would be in the classroom. You have to believe that all of the outstanding teachers of a grade level, in a department, or even in the building, know what good teaching looks like. They know when someone cannot carry the load.

It is very easy to stick your head in the sand (Ostrich Administration will be discussed later) and just let that person continue and, eventually, earn tenure. It is not easy to tell someone that their best effort is just not good enough. It is not easy to tell someone that you are not recommending that they return to the school as a teacher. But my friend, that is why you get the big bucks.

It is my strong belief, that the only thing harder would be to face your faculty down the road and talk of excellence, and talk of high standards and high expectations, and many of them know that you are full of fertilizer because look who you hire and worse, look who you eventually gave tenure to. It was just easier not to fire him or her. You cannot put yourself in these kinds of positions. *People remember!*

Not Yet

It is fairly traditional for the principal or superintendent to stand in front of the faculty at the opening of school or on the last day of school and say, *"This is the best faculty."* I have never stood in front of the faculty and said that it was the best faculty because they would know this is a lie. Everyone knows that we have a few teachers who are incompetent (I did hire a couple of them – I made mistakes). I have never said collectively that they are the best and sadly, I will never get to say it. This is because the two teachers I consider bordering on incompetency will not retire before I do. And I do not have strong enough grounds nor will the board of education file for their removal. There are not enough grounds to have them removed (even though my observations and evaluations have indicated my dissatisfaction with their performance and pedagogical abilities) and, therefore, in mass, this is not the *greatest* faculty.

And while we are on the topic, the difficulty of removing a tenured teacher from his or her position is like trying to push a filled cement truck up a forty five degree embankment with its parking brake on, motor off, and the transmission in reverse! That would be easier and more doable! In situations where even the concept of moving toward dismissal was just a notion by the board of education, it was eventually decided not to move forward due to the expense involved and the years it would take – if you won at all. The teacher would still be paid; however, he or she would be on administrative leave in a room in the central office. There would be the salary of the person hired to be the leave replacement for that teacher added into the costs and I haven't even mentioned legal fees!

Add to all that, the possibility that the district does not prevail and the teacher eventually returns to the classroom. Or the commissioner of education rules that the teacher will be suspended for a half year or a full year and then return. The removal of a teacher is a daunting task. Even the worst teacher you have in your building is still going to keep right on teaching due to tenure. The hamburger flipper at McDonalds who constantly misses the grill is fired, but someone attempting to educate children and is performing poorly stays. Why? There are two situations that hogtie principals. One is the power of the teachers' union protecting its weakest link. And two is the state education department and tenure laws make this as close to impossible as they can make it.

The state department of education and teachers' unions will not address the concept of teachers not being effective – that is your job.

Therefore, my strongest advice is to deny continuation of probation to everyone within the first two years who even remotely looks like they will not be *outstanding*. Having accepted this advice, know that as principal you could open your office window, stick your head out the window and whisper, *"I have a teaching vacancy"*, and within seconds you will have a hundred candidates throwing their resume at you. It is a buyer's market – the tenure system is stacked against you – so use the overflow of available teachers to your school's advantage.

I Can't Eat in that Restaurant Anymore

One of the slipperiest components of your job [**Grease Spot #40**] comes at hiring time, and this goes beyond the hiring of competent people. One issue I find most annoying is what I call, *I Can't Eat in that Restaurant Anymore*. Maybe it is just me, but time and time again, when people find out what I do for a living, I am beset with resumes and comments about a wonderful person who always wanted to be a teacher, who just graduated from college with a teaching degree, and would I *just give that person an interview, please? "Just for practice,"* I am always told.

Where does this come from? Only everywhere! Many years ago, my wife and I frequented a great little Italian restaurant. It was not a fancy place but was nice, clean, and reasonably priced with *great* food and the best Grandma Pizza on the planet! As my family and I became known there, due to the frequency of our visits, it wasn't long before we met the owner, who was also the chef. Our relationship became more special when I told him my son was going to culinary school and that I also loved to cook. Our discussions became more detailed, frequent, and comfortable. Each time we went there, it was like when Norm walked into Cheers.

As an outgrowth of our conversations, the chef learned that I was a school principal. A year or so down the road, he approached me with the resume of his daughter who would be finishing college later that spring and would be looking for a job. *All he wanted* was for me to look over her resume and to let him know if it was good and just interview her so she could practice being interviewed. Now, if you believe that was *all he wanted* for his little girl, I have a bridge I would like to sell you in Brooklyn. Maybe it was my imagination but the portions of food that my family and I received from that point on seemed larger, fresher and saucier! I ate well, my friends; *it was good to be king!* But I also knew that probably my meals in this restaurant were numbered.

So what did I do? I looked the resume over, made a change or two, and then handed it back to him the next time we went into the restaurant. He told me that she applied for a position in my district after seeing an advertisement in the paper. I interviewed her and found her lacking and, of course, she went no further in the process (looking for a n-a-t-u-r-a-l b-o-r-n t-e-a-c-h-e-r). Now, maybe I was wrong! Maybe the chef would be fine; he says he was, but I did not feel as warm as Norm, when a few weeks later we went to eat there again. I never went back to eat there again after that night. O.K. Maybe it is just me and my imagination, but the man whose daughter I didn't think highly enough to hire (and make her *set-for-life*) would be preparing food for me and my family. *What do you think?*

The person who hired me as a teacher in the school district where I eventually became a principal asked me to interview his wife for substitute teaching. I interviewed her and started to call her for substitute teaching jobs. A short-term leave came up unexpectedly, and I gave her the leave position that was to last six-weeks. As time went on and I saw her regularly, I realized that she was *terrible* and had *significant* problems controlling the class. Needless to say, she did not get a full-time job in the school the subsequent year, and he barely spoke to me again, *ever*, although we continued to work in the same school district for years.

Bring It On

Each spring comes the onslaught of friends, friends of friends, acquaintances, and friends of board of education members, sons or daughters of people throughout the county, all of whom want an interview for a special person. *"I am not asking for anything special or expect anything, but this is my _____'s resume, and would you mind......"* Honestly, a few of these have worked out very well but for each one that has, there are a dozen that did not resulting in a broken or bruised relationship. At this point, I tell anyone who asks what I do for a living that I am a field auditor for the Internal Revenue Service. That keeps most people away!

I *do not* count *not* hiring any of these people as a grease spot on the high-wire. In fact, had I hired any of them or the dozen or so like them, during my career, *that* would have been a grease spot because the faculty would know how they got hired or who they knew that got them hired, not what they knew and were capable of. And that would have been a huge credibility issue. *That is a greased wire!*

You really have only two choices: Commit yourself to being true to yourself and your commitment to excellence or just be a wonderful person and have a school filled with nice people who are friends of friends. My dining experience at that restaurant would have been significantly *and eternally* enhanced had I hired the chef's daughter. I would also have had a continuing positive relationship with a colleague who brought me to a school district that I love had I maintained his wife on staff. None of these things were easy and neither were the other ones I loathe to take space up in this book about. However, you might eat a little better and not get the cold shoulder from some people but I submit to you that the school would not be the kind of place you would want to work in or the kind of place you would want to send your own child to. And that must always be the bottom line.

So where will you draw the line? Will you interview anyone who knows a friend of yours? I certainly have hired a few outstanding teachers based upon recommendations of people I knew, people who knew people who knew people. I even hired the daughter of a good friend because she had the potential of being an outstanding teacher (both her parents, by the way, were teachers), but early on I was praying she would be good to save the friendship. And please do not get caught up in the philosophical rationalization about if the person who was prompting you to interview their friend's friend, or daughter, or wife, etc. that they will understand when you don't hire them. After all, remember, they just want you to interview them to give them practice at interviewing or for you to offer advice to this teacher new to the field. That they would understand this was just a courtesy interview. Bulldoggies! Wake up and smell the roses Pollyanna. In many cases, we are talking blood relatives, a force so emotional that it defies logic or reasoning. My suggestion is to recognize the slippery wire and consider anyone approaching you with *someone* as a potential grease source and *step carefully*.

You are going to lose friends. You are going to have people say, "Who does he or she think they are not hiring my _____?" The best advice I can give you is, well, really two bits of advice. One, hire the best no matter where they come from or who you may lose as a friend or acquaintance, and two, never tell the chef of your favorite restaurant what you do for a living. You can always get new friends, but a great Duck-a-l'Orange is hard to come by. And just so you understand *reality* when it comes up to you, I was *forced*, by a superintendent, to hire two people during my career.

And speaking of difficult situations, how about that substitute teacher who, for the past few years, has always been there for you in school and who you know that you can count on even at that very last minute to come in and cover a class? For whatever reason, he or she has been an *outstanding* substitute, but you know he or she does not have the day-to-day ability that you want in a classroom, and now he or she comes to you and wants to be considered for a full-time job. This has happened many, many times, and now you have to deliver the message: "You are a great substitute teacher and thank you for coming in whenever we call, but I have some reservations about your becoming a full-time, day-to-day teacher." And doing that is another reason why, my friend, you get the BIG bucks!

The easiest thing in the world would be to just say, "Sure, come onboard; you've been a great substitute teacher, and we owe you this job." The answer is a clear and resounding: *You don't owe anyone anything!* It is my responsibility to hire and place into the classrooms only outstanding educators. I look at it this way. As a principal, I gave you a chance to show me how good you are. I have given you regular and consistent opportunities – more so than most people just coming in for an interview.

Chapter 6

What Do These Parents Want Anyway?
Be Careful! Many of Them are Equipped with Grease Guns

Realistically, there is no way that your high-wire cannot be greased when it comes to working with parents [**Grease Spot #41**]. In most cases, it is lose-lose because you cannot prevent emotion entering into any of these situations. Parents want the best for their kids, and chances are pretty good that parents making their way to your office feel that something is not working *in their child's favor*. Very few come for the greater good of the organization. With all that is written about the woes of public schools, pointing accusatory fingers at administrators and teachers, too little is written or spoken about the lack or abdication of responsibility of parents. Three-quarters of all the ills associated with schooling can be easily, and I use the word *easily* on purpose, *easily* eradicated if parents weren't attempting to be their child's *friend* and instead would be their child's parent (and all of the responsibilities associated with that position).

The majority of parents are cooperative, reasonable, and supportive of the school. However, you, as principal, will be spending less time with these parents as you will with the other segment of parent population. That population, I refer to them as the No-Not-My-Kid Parents, are there to *protect* their child. As if any of us went into this business to do harm to children or young adults. As if any of us get up each morning and say, "Today, I am going to attempt to ruin the academic career of..."

I have been in many situations where a child has been seen by an adult in the school and/or has confessed to doing - *whatever*. I have picked up the phone to notify the parents of the situation surrounding the event, only to have the parent say to me, "O.K., well thank you, Dr. Sternberg, when ____ gets home I will talk with him/her to find out what *really* happened." And sure enough, the next morning mom or dad (and sometimes both) come into my office and tell their little cherub to tell me "what *really* happened." The parent then usually goes on to comment that "____ (their child) was not in the area, room, hallway, cafeteria, school, on campus, village, town, county, state, country, planet, or solar system when the incident occurred - and the adult witness saw it wrong. Now, Dr. Sternberg, I do not want any of this on my child's permanent record!"

Approaching the most irate parent calmly will probably defuse the issue somewhat. The grease is there. They are not removing it, and you lack the capability of removing it, so know it is there and step carefully. You know that without their complete satisfaction with *everything* you do and say, they are going the superintendent and/or your board of education. So the important issue is to get things right, say the right things, and do the right things. The foundational component to doing this is what I call the *Order of Logic*. Will your actions and your words to the student and/or parent stand the test of the *Order of Logic*?

The Order of Logic

Will *reasonable* people, sitting around a *reasonable* table, in a *reasonable* time period, view *your actions and words* as *reasonable*?

- Have you garnered enough information (and this is regardless of if this is a disciplinary action, a question about grades, or any issue about anything associated with your school that a parent might disagree with) and you have attempted to apply the wisdom of Solomon to the issue?

- Have you sought (depending on the issue) student input, teacher input, and/or parent input?

- Have you looked at the circumstances leading up to the situation?

- Have you reviewed (and are about to follow) the policies and procedures of your school/school district (and/or county, state or federal statutes)?

- Have you allowed some time to pass so that decisions are not made in the potential heat of the moment?

- Have you remained calm and not made the situation personal?

- Have you reviewed past issues involving the student, parents *and* the teacher(s) involved?

Touch-Base [Grease Spot # 42]

Your day will be crammed with many issues and responsibilities but the *touch-base* (your *need* - and I use the word *need* on purpose - to follow through after an issue in school that has involved a meeting with parents) is an imperative. I am referring to a follow-up phone call (touch-base) after a meeting with parents involving their child. For instance, you had a meeting with a parent about an issue with a teacher or another student and you did everything you needed to do to get the issue resolved.

It has now been a week and all is quiet. You now have the option of doing one of two things. You can just forget about the situation and move on *or* you can call the parent to see how things are going! In the margin of my planning calendar, I make a note for a week after *any meeting* I have with a parent, to call the parent and just ask, "*How is everything going since we last spoke?*" Please note, I do not ask if everything is O.K., I just note that I want to *touch-base* and see how things are going. This is a subtle, but in my mind a significant difference. What is really wonderful is when (and I do not mean to be disingenuous, just honest) I get the answering machine! I leave the same message as I would have delivered had I directly connected with the parent, but I get credit for the *touch-base*. *The onus is now on the parent to call me back if there continues to be an issue.* I would like to nominate for a Noble prize the inventor of the answering machine.

So, why is the *touch-base* so important? It demonstrates that you care and that the situation was not dismissed or forgotten by you. The parent now knows you are concerned enough to do a follow up. I have found it to be an excellent grain of sand added to my beach. Most parents are very impressed with the *touch-base*. I have reached out, noted my concern for a positive resolution, and now, if there continues to be an issue, the parent has to take the next step. It is a calculated yet win-win situation.

Here is a way to demonstrate that you are on top of important issues within the school, and to every parent that their issue is important to you because it is important to them. Do not fall into the grease spot of making judgments as to which is an important issue and which is not. If a parent has an issue, it must be seen and treated as important by you. This does not mean complete parent satisfaction, it just means that you have applied *due diligence* to *their* issue. I get about two return calls from parents out of every ten *touch-base* calls I make.

Partnerships

Developing partnerships between school personnel and families is one of the most effective methods for improving student effort and performance and is a clear degreaser of your high-wire. When the values and goals of administrators and teachers are reinforced at home, they quickly become ingrained in students, which can lead to fewer difficult students and improved academic success. The main reason to create school-home partnerships is to help all students succeed in school. The amount of time that we as school principals can spend with our students is obviously limited by the constraints of the school day. However, if we have parents who are advocates that are speaking the same language at home, it reinforces the message that is being delivered throughout the school day.

Students begin to see the importance of school because they are hearing about its importance both at school *and* at home. When parents hold school in high regard, students are more likely to as well. The attitude that students bring to the classroom is largely a result of the attitude about education that they hear at home. A difficult student who hates math and does not see the point of geometry likely has parents at home that feel that much of what goes on in a school is pointless. The attitude of these students can potentially be changed by changing the attitude of the parents. Staying in regular communication and building a sense of partnership can help bring the family around to the importance of what is being done in school.

We are all aware of the myriad of reasons why some parents stay away from school. As principal, you would like to believe that families are capable of supporting the importance of school without our help. However, this is simply may not be the case. As a school administrator, I have found parent engagement to be a question of balance. There are helicopter parents that are more than willing to be involved in the school setting as long as it directly impacts their child. They want to know everything and anything, all the time. On the other hand, attracting parents of poor students or those with disruptive behavior to the school can be difficult. Getting everyone under the tent to establish achievement and behavioral expectations is key, as parents need to understand and support the goals and expectations established for their child.

Reading Your Community

An effective anti-greasing measure on the high-wire involving parents and their involvement in your professional life is that you need to make sure you have been *extremely* proactive. Have you effectively communicated all the rules and expectations to parents in some type of written form and/or made parents informed (in writing) of where that information is easily accessible. It is critically important that at some point there needs to be access to you to discuss these rules and procedures so that they remain current and parents feel involved.

As you *read* your community and get to understand its underpinnings and form a picture of the parents' needs, have you attempted to establish links from school to home and from home to school? By keeping parents informed, a sense of trust will grow. As principal, utilize ongoing, proactive *reach-outs* to parents via the phone, meetings, letters, emails, and other technology. By using multi-modality practices, you will help to ensure that you are reaching the broadest range of parents. Using native language awareness and sensitivity can build a huge amount of trust even by just your attempt to do so. Share strategies for parents to use at home through pamphlets, flyers, and links to neighborhood social service outlets and agencies that provide support and direction. Plan on a recognition and/or some encouragement opportunity for parents for being involved, showing interest, or demonstrating support for their children's school. Efforts to make your school accessible and transparent go a long way to easing suspicions. The fact is: Reality is one thing, and perception is another, and to many people, *perception is reality*. Perception [**Grease Spot #43**] can be a grease-causing agent!

Also, it is imperative that teachers be in contact with parents throughout the school year, not just when they have a problem but at times when the child is performing well. A quick phone call to comment positively on a child's performance will open many doors so that parents feel free to share their frustrations, challenges and ask questions. What you want is a partnership, and that takes more than just communicating or hosting parent nights. It takes an effort by parents and staff to develop relationships. It is your responsibility to create an ethos where teachers regularly reach out to the parents of students in their class.

When teachers and principals have relationships with parents, it is easier for everyone to share. Often, I have found these relationships will allow parents to ask questions, share advice, and will often lead to effective interventions to support children. An effective rule-of-thumb is that teachers should reach out to a quarter of the parents of their kids every month. That results in about three unsolicited, touch-base phone calls to the parent(s) of each kid a year. *You*, however, must make the first step and probably the second, third, fourth, and so on to make this happen.

Establishing a Level Playing Field

Establishing a level playing field is something that you will want to accomplish for both students and teachers. Certainly, your moral obligation is primarily to the students within your school. How do you establish a level playing field for all students who enter your building regardless of their social, economic, or tangential educational experiences prior to reaching your school?

As a principal, you cannot make up for years of both educational and social neglect in the short time students will be in your care. Realistically, you cannot change what has taken place before and the influences on a particular child. However, I believe it is incumbent upon you to take the necessary steps to create a level playing field for everyone. What does this translate to? In each school this will be different. Here again, reading the needs of the community and its stakeholders will be instrumental in assisting the students in your school.

I cannot buy into the, *it takes a whole village to raise a child* concept. I fully understand the roots of the saying, but much has been lost in translation. It is a copout to ask *the village* to stand-in for parent responsibilities. Too many parents are waiting for too long for *the village* to do what they do not want to do: *take responsibility for their children*.

You and Your Parent-Teacher Organization
The Potential Grease Spot that Keeps Moving

Some of the most dynamic and spirited leaders that principals will encounter are PTA, PTO, or 6-12 presidents. Their spirited desire to do good for the children is, at times, so emotionally centered that a principal will need to be very careful and skillful as he or she sets out to create a professional relationship. This spot on the high-wire can easily become *very* greasy [**Grease Spot #44**]. That understanding should prompt you to speak with your parent organization president(s) two, possibly three times per week. This repetitive contact creates an established relationship so that if and when the yogurt-is-about-to-hit-the-fan, familiarity allows for uninhibited dialogue because you do communicate so frequently. This effort will need to be ongoing, as each year new presidents come onboard. The culture of your relationship with the leaders is *usually* and hopefully passed along with ownership and control of the presidential gavel.

Relationships with Students

Your high-wire is very greasy [**Grease Spot #45**] if the students do not, at least, respect you. One thing I have not commented on is the importance of *listening to students*. One of the important things I do as I wander from classroom to classroom is to stop and ask kids three questions:

1) *What are you doing?*

2) *Why are you doing it?*

3) *How do you think you will be able to use this outside of the classroom?*

Of course, I do this while the kids are working independently or in small, cooperative learning groups, not while the teacher is teaching to the entire class.

Your relationship with students is the most fascinating aspect of being a principal *and the most fun!* You are truly many things to many people and all of those are wrapped up in how you work with kids. There will be times that you will need to be mother, father, aunt, uncle, friend, disciplinarian, rabbi, priest, ombudsperson, supporter, cheerleader, rule maker, protector, and advisor. There will be times when you will be a few of these things at the same time. One day you will be cheering a student on as he or she attempts to sink the winning basket, or score the winning goal, or perform in the school musical, and the day before or the very next day after, you might be suspending him or her for an offense that requires a consequence.

How you play each role and even more importantly, how you transition between all of your roles with individual kids will be extremely important and telling. Always remember, kids never forget how they were treated!

The vast majority of kids know the difference between right and wrong, between making good choices and not thinking about their action prior to doing something. I believe there is an expectation on their part that there will be a consequence for their negative action. How you transition is important. So you have suspended Billy for an infraction of the school's code of conduct. He does his two-day suspension, returns to school on Thursday. You conduct your usual re-entry meeting first thing in the morning prior to his first class period. Thursday night is a basketball game and Billy is one of the starting five on the team. Regardless if the team wins or does not, when you see him in the hallway between classes on Friday (and I would suggest to go as far as purposefully looking for him), at a quiet time when none of his friends are around, give him a fast but sincere, "you played a good game last night."

Billy now knows you have seen him in a different light. It was you and him, one on one. If you try to do this in front of his friends, you might be rebuffed because he needs to maintain his credibility (cred) with his peers, but you would be surprised how positive his reaction will be when you do reach out to him and he knows you also see him in a different light - and the next time you need to deal with Billy about a discipline manner, you might be surprised (pleasantly so) about where your relationship now is.

On the elementary level your mere recognition, gentle smile, and/or passing "hello" will be seen as a major event for kids. The lower the grade, the more momentous the recognition. Use all of this to your advantage. Regardless of the age, students (children and young adults) respond well to recognition. Selecting time and place is extremely important as well as being able to *work* the occasion.

It is All About the Presentation

Students know when they have done something wrong. While they might not like the consequence, *they do expect it*. How the consequence is presented is important on many levels. It should not be seen as vindictive nor should it seem to them that you are enjoying and savoring the moment. There needs to be a logical relationship between what has occurred and the scope of the consequence; they should be logically related and something students can understand. The student does not have to accept the consequence, but he or she does have to understand why this certain consequence was linked to their action. They were not bad kids, just kids making poor choices.

It is important for you to learn how you can assist a student in processing what is happening after he or she has broken a school rule. Parents will rally to the defense of their child and, at times, go to unreasonable lengths. They fear the dubious *permanent record* that they think will trail their child - forever. Parents who feel they need to defend their child's actions rather than taking a more parental, disciplinary role will prove to be one of your biggest problems in working with their child.

I believe, unfortunately, that most parents will not be on your side - the school's side. This does not serve their child well. The best you can probably hope for is a level of understanding that you will be delivering a less severe consequence *this time,* with an understanding that if something like this happens again, the consequences will be more severe. In this manner, you are getting the parents to assist you in monitoring their child's behavior going forward. In many ways, you have gotten them on your side, albeit reluctantly because they know future consequences and fear that outcome.

A disciplined environment is highly important. I am not advocating an overly strict disciplinary environment but rather an environment where teachers are free to teach and students are free to learn in a safe, orderly school where behavioral norms are clearly understood by all, adhered to, and enforced in a fair and consistent manner. I believe the aim is to create within all students, self-discipline and the ability to solve problems rather than to just provide consequences in response to misbehavior. Not an easy task when each classroom teacher may have their own discipline tolerance level and their own established rules based upon those tolerances.

Student Discipline

It would be impossible to try to fit into any tome practical advice about working with students in a disciplinary manner. So much of what has to be known includes knowing the students in your school, their family backgrounds, and the degree of support can you *reasonably* expect from home. The home component is the wild card [**Grease Spot #46**]. However, the bottom line is that your high-wire will have prescribed amounts of grease depending on whether your school is perceived as well disciplined in terms of student behavior. Are kids safe in school from other kids, and how do you go about achieving an ethos of proactive discipline as well as self-discipline with realistic, measured discipline complemented by effective consequences?

Having Zero Tolerance for Zero Tolerance Policies

There should be zero tolerance for zero tolerance (ZT) policies in schools. A lockstep approach to disciplinary consequences mandated by most ZT policies creates more of a penal system in schools than one that reflects sound pedagogical practices. Our children deserve the discretion and good judgment that principals should bring to every situation. Automatically meting out punishment and, in most cases, severe punishments as called for by most ZT policies, flies in the face of logic, reason, and foundational educational underpinnings of how students should be treated within a school. According to the blog Delaware Liberal (2009), under ZT "School administrators are barred from using their judgment, reducing severe punishments to be proportional to minor offenses, or considering extenuating circumstances. Consequently, these policies are sometimes derided as zero-intelligence policies." The application of one-size-fits-all consequences for the most insignificant offense flies in the face of developing consequences based upon a spiraling progression of severity based upon a student-centered set of needs.

Administration and boards of education can have zero tolerance for certain actions of a student or groups of students against others in a school. However, when that tolerance level results in a mandated set of predetermined consequences without school-based discretion ZT is irrational. The relationship between the student who brings a Boy Scout knife to school to show classmates, the one who brings a knife to school because he or she feels threatened, and the student who comes to school with a blade to inflict premeditated bodily harm, are three hands in the same card game with each requiring different treatment. However, under most zero tolerance policies, all three would be treated equally and equally as harshly. ZT policies treat a kindergarten student and a twelfth grade student equally. Discipline issues must be looked at as an equitability issue and not all punishments should be equal as ZT policies tend to mandate.

The term *zero tolerance* is the hook that is used to hang a disciplinary consequence (mandated punishment) on and has a tendency to make lay people feel more comfortable, even making them feel more protected. However, administrators need to reject any system where the punishment at first glance appears just, but as situational judgment is removed, what appears as a swift sword of justice ends up impaling those who require alternative consequences. The automatic suspension, expulsion, and/or calling the police, all of which have at their nucleus predetermined ZT sanctions, means the abdication of administrative judgment. It is too easy to just recite the zero tolerance mantra that removes student age, intent, behavioral history, and the circumstances surrounding the event. In reality, there is no credible evidence that zero tolerance reduces student violence or drug abuse (Skiba, 2000; *American Psychologist*, 2008).

The Feather or Shotgun Approach

We administrators have been well schooled in efforts and practices designed to raise assessment scores as well as directly influence classroom instruction. Our sometimes myopic lens may prevent us from seeing other than results of Annual Yearly Progress [AYP] data, indicators of levels of proficiency on state exams, graduation rates, and student acceptance rates to two- or four-year colleges. One glaring omission in this landscape is how best to determine fair, consistent, and effective disciplinary practices.

How can we be proactive and use preemptive measures to thwart, minimize and/or eliminate potential discipline issues that might require us to follow a school district's ZT policy?

How do we take the temperature of a school?

What are the indicators of a student with growing issues?

How do principals learn and apply good common sense efforts that are fair, firm and effective?

How much do principals know about fair discipline commensurate with a student's age, action, and intent?

A major part of the ZT issue and one that might even seem, at first blush, to fly in the face of the anti-zero tolerance movement is that many administrators are too lenient in dealing with discipline. Also, there are insufficient proactive interventions and perhaps poorly planned and applied consequences. As a result, larger, more complicated issues develop that are then met with ZT policies. Therefore, in terms of discipline, many times principals utilize a feather in an attempt to bring down a charging rhinoceros and then a shotgun to get the fly.

Proactive

Administrative capacity to be proactive is somewhat restricted by a number of factors. These factors include parental cooperation and support, the culture of the community, the availability of human resources like psychologists, social workers, and trained guidance counselors, the tendencies and preconceived notions of the staff, and finally the school climate which accepts certain behavioral patterns as common to the environment and as being inevitable for certain children and young adults.

Removing a student from school might initially appear as an effective alternative. However, we have been suspending students from school for decades and those students, when returned to school, are rarely effectively matriculate into becoming a productive member of school society. When poor choices or lose emotional balance (and the resulting behavior) is treated as equal to premeditated acts, then the educational system is failing that child or young adult. As principals know that differentiating instruction for students is needed for learning, why have administrators fallen so short when they make the assumption that a ZT policy will, therefore, address the behavioral needs of all students?

There exists zero tolerance "traps" (Horner, et.al, 2000). As identified by Horner, et al. (2000), these traps in the zero tolerance mindset are getting tough is enough, looking for a quick fix, finding one powerful trick, and believing more is better. Effective discipline solutions are many times multidisciplinary in practice and are most effective when met with incremental consequences.

What are the Alternatives?

Prevention is the best management tool. It is critically important that principals address high-risk factors. Principals must be aware of whether members of diverse racial groups as well as students of various ethnic backgrounds, religious preferences, and sexual orientations feel that the population (both student and staff) of the school treat them fairly and view them as equals. Developing an awareness of who is being targeted or bullied is essential for prevention.

What adult in the school is looking for the student who feels rejected or persecuted and, as a result, comports themselves in a socially withdrawn and isolate manner? Is there sensitivity to and a mechanism in place to pick up on students with low interest in school and academics and who demonstrate atypical social behaviors? Who are the drug users and the gang members in the school? Of most importance, are the avenues for students to share their concerns with their principal seen as non-intimidating. Creating an environment that supports and sustains positive relations between staff members and youngsters and working together with students to develop positive relationships through participation in peer mediation and conflict resolution programs are crucial and significant first steps toward preventative measures. The involvement of the adults in the life of the child into the process is also critical.

Providing youngsters with an alternative to the poor choices they could potentially make is a good preventative measure. The development of skill-building techniques through social skills programs as well as preemptive role playing behavioral actions to various confrontations that a student might have will be helpful as well. Marshal all of the resources not only in school but in the community as well to focus on the troubled youth. Interventions are generally most effective if they start early in a student's school career, are long term in scope, and tend to stick with the student even as the student transfers between elementary and secondary levels. By targeting some children as potential problems and supporting them during their K-12 school experience, administrators could essentially be replacing the need for zero tolerance responses.

In-school suspension coupled with behavioral support from social workers, school psychologist, guidance staff, etc. for behavioral management programs is a strong option. Community service intervention, alternative schools/classes, parental involvement to a point where they can be coached in how to work with their disruptive child along with social support in terms of peer counseling can be an effective option.

Zeroing in on the Bottom Line

Zero tolerance policies are contrary to logical practices that administrators have always relied on to redirect inappropriate social behaviors. They fail to take into account what you, as a principal, would know about a particular student as well as your knowledge of adolescent or pre-adolescent behavior patterns.

We cannot allow ourselves to assume that removing students from an educational environment based upon solely punitive zero tolerance mandates will be good for that child or the other the children of the school. Zero Tolerance is an impulse reaction; it is not a deterrent or remedy. The belief that fast action is superior to deliberation is misguided.

Cultural Diversity

Where we come from does set the platform for how we interpret the world but that doesn't mean a cultural background *limits* perceptions. We all have choices in life, including how we view the world.

Principals and teachers should be culturally responsive and competent as schools and classrooms become increasingly linguistically and culturally diverse. Teachers and principals should understand important ways in which cultures differ and how this can influence student behavior. This knowledge will enable you and your teachers to avoid some of the problems that surface each day. If teachers and principals are to become effective cross-cultural communicators, it is necessary to understand the role that culture plays in a school. Lustig and Koester (2003) define culture as "a learned set of shared interpretations about beliefs, values, and norms, which affect the behaviors of a relatively large group of people" (p. 9). Likewise, Samovar and Porter in their book Intercultural Communication (1982) explain culture as a medium that touches and alters all aspects of human life, including personality, how people express themselves (including displays of emotion), the way they think, how they move, and how problems are solved. When you and your teachers understand the cultural differences of your students, you will more likely respect diverse students and know how to guide them toward academic and personal success and fulfillment.

Bias is a tough, ongoing issue educators have long encountered, and it will continue to be [**Grease Spot #47**]. With the influx of several cultural subgroups, such as race, gender, or socioeconomic status, maintaining a school ethos that reaches all students *and their families* has become an even more complicated task. Successful principals will make *every* stakeholder group feel welcomed.

Students and their families have differing needs and multiple perspectives that should be respected so that students learn to honor each other's unique views and needs. This is especially critical for elementary students. Provide an environment where students learn to recognize each other's differences and respect them. Therefore, as younger students progress through school, they can understand and appreciate what different cultures have to offer and what is becoming the *tapestry* of the United States as opposed to a melting pot. One important way teachers can help students learn tolerance in a multicultural setting is by example, but first educators must overcome their own biases.

Home Sweet Home

As previously noted, developing partnerships between teachers, principals, and families is an effective method to improve student performance. Education can be the escape route out of poverty for many of our students. Those who dream of being the next multi-million dollar rock star or professional athlete and whose parents support that dream as opposed to the reality of what a quality education can provide need to be brought home to reality with their child. When the values and goals of the school are reinforced at home, they quickly become ingrained in the student. The foundational reason to establish partnerships is to help all students succeed in school *and* in later life. There are many students who do not see the correlation between school success and career success.

The attitude that your students bring to the classroom is largely a result of the attitude about education that they hear at home. The bottom line for me has always been and will always be - parents. Children are taught to hate, mistrust, and be prejudiced against others in their homes - *by their parents*. Their attitude can potentially be changed if you can change the attitude of the parents. Staying in constant communication and building a sense of partnership is the best vehicle to accomplishing this.

We hope families will support the importance of school, but "The family needs more help today because the family is no longer in control of all of the information and all the forces that impinge on the child" (Comer, 2004, p. 9). It becomes part of our role as teachers to help families support their children to give them a better chance of success in school. It is through these relationships we are able to help strengthen the message that the family is giving to the children which will then play a large role in improving the student's beliefs about school.

Multicultural

Multicultural education involves presenting opportunities in the classroom that value diversity and represents it in a positive manner. More specifically, ethnicity and race, class, and socioeconomic status, gender and sexual orientation, exceptionality, language, religion, geography and age need to be considered for students to understand the cultural backgrounds of others and to help eradicate the negative effects of biases. The essential elements of multicultural education require understanding of culture, cultural identity, pluralism, equality, and social justice. Culture encompasses shared attitudes, values, goals, and practices that characterize a specific group and, more significantly, how individuals in cultural groups are identified by their shared traits and values that are considered cultural identity. Pluralism refers to the smaller groups within a larger society who maintain their unique cultural identities. Equality is a result of believing that all cultural groups are equal and all have the same societal benefits which is closely associated with social justice, the principle that society should provide for those citizens who are not as privileged as others. These seemingly simple yet profound concepts are not as universally accepted as they should be and can be a significant grease spot [**Grease Spot #48**].

By 2052, children of color and Hispanics will comprise nearly half of the American school-aged population. In addition, with the increasing number of immigrants and multicultural groups in America, it is imperative that educators learn and understand the needs of all students to make them feel included. Instructional strategies that address cultural diversity have to be incorporated so that both students and teachers have a better understanding of cultural diversity and the negative effect of societal prejudices. Equality can only occur when students and teachers respect other cultures.

Multicultural education can help to create a generation of students who are more tolerant and treat others with equality. The diversity of a global society requires that students interact positively with others. Multicultural education involves positive modeling and integration of the different groups that people belong to with an emphasis on ethnicity, race, religion, class, and gender. It may also extend into intellectual and physical abilities. It is essential for teachers to be sensitive and empathetic to their students' values and backgrounds in order for students to achieve learning goals, regardless of the subject. It cannot be assumed by you, as principal, that your teachers enter their classrooms with the training, understanding, and knowledge necessary when it comes to multicultural education. That assumption creates a huge potential and explosive grease spot.

Effective Practices

The question that you will need to ask yourself is, *how do leaders implement effective practices in a culturally diverse organization?* The current climate impacts educational leaders because they now, more than ever, have to be aware of multicultural diversity. There may need to be a tremendous shift in how we treat individual students that walk through your halls. Principals can no longer expect culturally diverse students to conform to the current traditions of the school. Schools must instead conform, to some reasonable degree, to the traditions of the whole. Effective principals will handle this by identifying all diversities in the school and then do their best, and to the degree reasonably possible, to include their customs and traditions into daily routines.

I offer the following list of books that schools can utilize to help complete a circle of cultural awareness. It is best to stay away from the "_____ Day" or "_____ Month" recognitions/celebrations because then cultural diversity is not *part of your daily* school experience, it is a day or month celebration - and then what?

There are many ways to make your school diverse. One of the best ways, I believe, is to have a class library (on the elementary level) and/or a school library full of books that celebrate diversity. Cultural experiences through books can easily be interwoven into existing unit themes throughout the year.

Umbrella by Taro Yashima
Bringing the Rain to the Kapiti Plain by V. Aardema
Gilberto and the Wind by Marie Hall Ets
The Story of Ping by Marjorie Flack
Elmer, the Patchwork Elephant by David McKee

Katy No Pocket by Emmy Payne
Birthdays! Celebrating Life Around the World by Eve B. Feldman
Children Just Like Me by Barnabas and Anabel Kindersley
Everybody Eats Bread by J. Powell
Activities, Projects, and Inventions from Around the World by M. Kohl & J. Potter
The Kids' Multicultural Art Book: Art and Craft Experiences from Around the World by Alexandra Terzian
Ben's Trumpet by Rachel Isadora
A Birthday Basket for Tia by Pat Mora
Bright Eyes, Brown Skin by Cheryl Willis Hudson & Bernette Ford
A Chair for My Mother by Vera Williams
Everybody Cooks Rice by Norah Dooley
Families Are Different by Nina Pellegrini
Friends at School by Rochelle Bunnett
Hats, Hats, Hats by Ann Morris
Hello, Amigos! By Tricia Brown
Jamaica Tag-Along by Juanita Havill
Just Us Women by Jeannette Caines
Kindergarten Kids by Ellen B. Senisi
The Land of Many Colors by The Klamath County YMCA Family Preschool
Loin Dancer: Ernie Wan's Chinese New Year by Kate Waters & Madeline Slovenz-Low
Mama, Do You Love Me? By Barbara M. Joosse
The Patchwork Quilt by Valerie Flournoy
Peek-a-Boo by Roberta Grobel Intrater
Say Hola to Spanish by Susan Middleton Elya
The Story of Ruby Bridges by Robert Coles
This is the Way We Go to School by Edith Baer
Together We Are Together by St. Brigid's Head Start Children
Too Many Tamales by Gary Soto & Ed Martinez
Two Eyes, a Nose, and a Mouth by Roberta Grobel Intrater
We Are All Alike….We Are Different by The Cheltenham Elementary School Kindergarten
Pepita Talks Twice by Ofelia Dumas Lachtman
Persepolis: The Story of a Childhood by Marjane Satrapi
Papa Tells Chita a Story by Elizabeth Fitzgerald Howard
Cocoa Ice by Diana Appelbaum
Experanza Rising by Pam Munoz Ryan
Amelia's Road by Linda Jacobs Altman and Enrique O. Sanchez
Aunt Flossie's Hats by Elizabeth Fitzgerald Howard and James
Amazing Grace by Mary Hoffman
Freedom Crossing by Margaret Goff Clark
Brave as a Mountain Lion by Ann Herbert Scott and Glo Coalgon
Pink and Say by Patricia Polacco
Mr. Lincoln's Way by Patricia Polacco

Mrs. Katz and Tush by Patricia Polacco
Chicken Sunday by Patricia Polacco
A Sweet Smell of Roses by Angela Johnson and Eric Valasquez
Beatrice's Goat by Page McBrier
The House on Mango Street by Sandra Cisneros
The Lotus Seed by Sherry Garland
All the Colors of the Earth by Sheila Hamanaka
The Crayon Box that Talked by and
Math Games & Activities From Around The World by Claudia Zaslavsky
One Green Apple by Eve Bunting
Chicken Chasing Queen of Lamar County by Janice Harrington
The Golden Rule by Ilene Cooper
Say Something by Peggy Moss
The Kite Runner by Khaled Hosseini
Bodega Dreams by Ernesto Quinonez
Down These Mean Streets by Piri Thomas
How the Garcia Girls Lost Their Accents by Julia Alvarez
Drown by Junot Diaz
Krik Krak by Edwidge Dandicat
Lucy by Jamaica Kincaid

Multicultural education should not focus on a week or month celebration of a specific ethnic group. Instead, multicultural education should be integrated into all subjects to present diverse cultural groups' history, culture, economics, sociology, and geography as well as holidays and languages. If your current curriculum focuses only on mainstream culture and the larger minority groups of African American and Hispanics, then you are lacking.

Working with Diverse Cultures – Grease is Grease No Matter How You Translate It

In my opinion (and an emotional one at that) the conditions matter less than whether the teacher *cares* about students. Certainly, the teacher must be competent and knowledgeable of the subject matter and classroom management, but what matters most, to children is whether the teacher *cares* about them. A teacher can draw up the most brilliant lesson plans and deliver them with eloquence, but none of it will make much of a difference if the teacher doesn't *appear* to care about the students [**Grease Spot #49**]. Some principals would probably say effective teaching is hitting all the marks on my performance evaluation, or effective teaching can be measured by how well a class is managed. I would add the need for a teacher to call home to check on students when they are absent, taking time to get to know students, sending notes home to commend children for good behavior or academic effort or achievement, and encouraging them to keep trying after a failure matter most to students and parents. When students know a teacher cares, that is when effective teaching has the best chance (and I would submit, *the only chance*) to occur and have a significant impact.

The professional development opportunities on cultural awareness and student learning styles that can be offered to staff are endless. But perhaps the best method you can use to foster a program that embraces diversity is to create programs that invite diverse members of the community to participate in school functions and programs – creating an open climate where there is an exchange of ideas between all stakeholders. Modeling sensitivity *consistently* and reinforcing the dignity of the individual is a good first step. Working to understand the culture, supporting employees or students who promote culture in a healthy way, and holding cultural expression up as an example are all helpful strategies for promoting awareness and sensitivity.

As an elementary school principal, I *get them* pretty young and innocent. None of them were born with prejudice against anyone – not even to the doctor that hit them on the bottom to get them going. I am continually amazed (and terrified, at times) to hear what comes out of the mouths of our young children. The origins and continuity of prejudice is a *learned concept* and, as you know, we do not teach it in school. Educators have an uphill battle but please understand, as a principal, where most prejudices develop and persevere over time and the subsequent battle that you must continue to fight. It can be very confusing for some children to see and hear one thing at home and the antithesis at school but that is the one time I want them to be confused *because it means they are listening.*

The Divide

Culturally, I think arriving at a fuller appreciation for others can be elusive, especially between groups with historical animosities. I'm not sure whether this is entirely the job of a school principal, but certainly you are in an important position of influence to help promote provocative, meaningful and respectful opportunities for discussion of key issues that define conflict between groups. I think this can be accomplished in schools through appropriate use of classroom time, such as integrating projects and learning experiences that allow for deeper consideration of culturally-based themes, across history, ELA, art, music, etc. The principal can challenge (cover word for *insist*) faculty to prioritize integration of such themes into the curriculum, as well as into extracurricular offerings.

Depending on what part of Oz the tornado lands you in, get the lay of the land by regularly meeting with stakeholders and moving forward to create a strong educational setting will be your responsibility. Cultural differences need to be considered, *embraced,* and used to the advantage of everyone. However, and I caution you, if it is just one month a year or one week or a year or a special holiday once a year – you will get nowhere. You need to make it part of the culture of your school.

You will, at times, be called upon to possibly negotiate between two divergent cultural perspectives within your school. Please understand that how you handle this situation will go a long way to you being seen as fair and consistent. As the principal, I would encourage the parties involved in the divergent cultural perspectives to present their opinions to one another. I don't necessarily believe that I would have to make decisions as to which was more appropriate because I do not want a dominant culture appearing to emerge based upon a principal's decision. Collaborating about differing preconceptions and assumptions could create a new perspective that could be used as a teamwork approach within an organization.

Student Assessment

There are three essential questions, I believe, that will enable you to transform your school into a focused professional learning community:

1. *What do we want students to learn?*
2. *How do we know students are learning?*
3. *What do we do when we find out students are not learning?*

There is no one way to know students are learning. The measurement instruments that we use should be varied. I have witnessed "C" students demonstrate a greater understanding and utilization of information than students who got all the answers correct on a formative assessment. So, students should be given multiple opportunities and ways to demonstrate what they have learned.

When students are not learning, we (teachers and you) must look at ourselves to determine what we need to change in order to ensure learning takes place. Once we have assessed what needs to change, we must research strategies and methods that have been proven to work in similar settings. After analyzing the information, you must act by implementing what we have learned collectively and individually.

There are a several options when out your students are not learning. You first must find out *why* they are not learning. Did they not understand the material, the teacher, or the teaching method? Were they just not interested and engaged in the material? Or maybe there was something outside of school that had them preoccupied? Either way, you must find out the reason and then address and correct the situation. Again, you must gain input and suggestions from your teachers. Since teachers are the ones closest to the students and know them best, they can guide your decisions about what changes might work. You could possibly make changes in procedures in class or even provide the teachers with the supplies and training they may need to be more successful.

I put a great deal of value in assessing how *we* are doing. I also come back to a true measure of learning as being able to bring something to life, project-based performance, presentations, demonstrations – and a lot less dependency on standardized assessment data. This is much more effective than a written test because I always believe, somewhat tongue-in-cheek, that the more one studies for a paper-and-pencil test the more quickly one will forget all the information they were just tested on.

Standardize

One way to maintain a grease-free high-wire is terms of teacher performance is the standardization of classroom practice. Writing it and saying it are the easy part - now try and accomplish it [**Grease Spot #50**]!

I think you would want to standardize common practices that were grounded in pedagogical research. I would also want the faculty to identify common essential learning outcomes for students on the same grade level and/or course. These outcomes should be standardized to ensure that all students have *access to the same learning opportunities*. Think level playing field.

To me, these are elements of the science of teaching. I would not want to standardize the art of teaching which is where each teacher's creativity and individualism is highlighted. If we are working towards the same goal, how we get there does not need to be exactly the same, *as long as* we all get there.

Someone said, *if you always do what you have always done, you will keep on getting the same results* (think Groundhog Day – the movie). As I look at the task before me as principal, I have no desire to reinforce the status quo. As a result of the attempt by schools to meet the minimum requirements of the *ridiculous* No Child Left Behind (2001) and now the even *more ridiculous* Race to the Top (2009); far too many classrooms are already standardized. Teachers teach the tested curriculum, and they ignore research-based practices and creativity. How many times has a student come up to a teacher and asked, *"Is this the right way to do this?"* or *"How do you want me to do this?"* This is because the standardized assessments require the one correct way of responding. Those two statements by students send shivers up and down my spine! Talk about the death of creativity, it signals the death of asking kids to think!

My desire as a principal is to influence teachers to think about why they are using common practices that yield certain results, instead of evidence-based practices that yield far reaching, cognitive developing and enhancing results.

It concerns me that according to Theodore Kaniuka (2009), children are being taught to pass the basic skills of state mandated assessments (and soon to come federally mandated assessments via Race to the Top) at the expense of other subjects like science and social studies that would aid in preparing students for careers or college. In an effort to appear that we are educating them (great assessment scores), we are actually short changing them when they don't receive an enhanced, higher cognitive curricula.

Data

I feel the same way about data that I do about a ninety-nine degree day with ninety-eight percent humidity - hate it but there is little I can do about it! If we accept the research of Arno Bellack (as cited in Lunenburg & Orenstein, 2004), data suggest that classrooms are "teacher dominated, subject centered, and fact oriented", and that, "as a teacher, you need to break this cycle of teaching" (p. 532). If we wish to move students to *inquiry learning, higher cognitive learning with authentic assessment*, you need students asking questions, moving beyond the facts and into relevancy modes of fact interpretation and usage. Unfortunately, even data comes into this equation because you need the data to know where you have been, where you are, and if you are where you want to be.

Might I suggest setting up a *Data Team* in your school? This team would consist of the principal, test coordinator, and possibly three to four teachers. The team adheres to a continuous improvement cycle as they examine patterns and trends, and establish specific timelines, roles, and responsibilities to facilitate analysis that results in performance-based action. The team asks the following questions in determining which data to use for analysis.

How do you (classroom teachers) use data to inform instruction and improve student achievement?

How do you (the classroom teacher) determine which data are the most important to use, analyze, or review?

In the absence of data, what is used as a basis for instructional judgment?

This sounds like a powerful team, doesn't it!

As principals we must be careful because in many ways we are using assessment scores (data) in ways they were never meant to be interpreted. The use of the *numbers* drives program changes, how we work with kids and many times where kids are *placed* or at minimum, what and how they are *expected* to learn. You should never consider them to be a major part of the *how are our kids doing* schema or are they any indicator of how a school is doing. It is too easy and becoming too prolific to hide behind the numbers.

Assessment scores are only one piece of the picture. Go ahead and laugh at me, but in some ways daily attendance rates of students is a better indicator of how a school is doing, as it represents how important parents think it is to come to school. The motivation to come to school has never been addressed, and in my mind tends to better address the *knowledge gained* factor because families and kids are voting with their feet.

As we work more closely with the data (which I totally disagree with as I was *never* labeled with some insidious number as a student and am the better for it) we are developing a model in some districts that basically ignores the Level 3 and 4 students (they do well enough on their own, and will be fine) and focus on moving the Level 2s to 3s, and providing intervention for the Level 1s and some low 2s. This is an *statistically* effective theory that targets the right kind and level of resources to where they can make a difference. I am not sure, however, that placing kids in Levels will show a high correlation with graduating life-long learners who contribute well to society [**Grease Spot #51**]. Accumulation of points is not an indicator of what students know or can do. Labeling learners (a product of NCLB) stunts growth and limits creativity.

Great Questions

Ask yourself the following:

If you abolished all tests, what would you use to measure learning?

What would be the limitations of your method? What would be the advantages?

How would you know if it measured worked what students have learned?

Talk about some great questions to toss out at a faculty meeting!

As a principal, you will need to understand the place of and your ability to *mine* data and effectively use data [**Grease Spot #52**]. For example, use evidence-based teaching strategies. We need to track individual and group performance and use data to target instructional interventions, reassess and target additional interventions until all students demonstrate success. This is a TEAM event (think Data Team involving teachers, special education staff, administration, and other experts as required).

You facilitate and create the conditions where educators collaboratively look at data (performance, perceptual, and achievement data), to isolate positive and negative trends so that improvements can be made to ensure that all students learn. In this sense, your role is to create a learning community of professionals (Data Team) dedicated to continuous improvement. I am not sure every classroom teacher needs to be a data expert (hence the Data Team). However, every teacher needs to understand how to interpret the data and/or at least understand what to do with the interpretation once presented to them.

Measurement

You must ensure that the teaching of the curriculum is carried out properly using multiple deliveries and containing differentiated instruction that meets the needs of all the students. In many schools, educational leaders evaluate student responses to indicate the effectiveness of the curriculum and its delivery. This is certainly a growing concept throughout our nation. In terms of student performance, it seems that test results are the focus, rather than whether or not students are *really* learning. It is hard to say what is good enough because "there is little concern about whether students can critically think or solve problems, or whether their social, personal, and emotional needs are being met" (Lunenberg & Ornstein, 2004, p. 472). It is not clear if teaching to the test, and the outcomes of these tests, are truly enough to evaluate student skills. What is sufficient may be to evaluate not only tests, but also a more well–rounded portfolio of student products, such as in–class performance, emotional well-being, writing samples, and other informal measurements.

Portfolio assessment is an ongoing authentic assessment. The authentic assessment involves the collection of all students' ongoing performance, including writing samples, presentations, authentic class performance, class observation, homework, and any other work that reflects student learning. The advantages of portfolio assessment are all the student learning samples are collected during authentic learning context and reflect students' real learning. The limitation is it is time consuming for a teacher to collect and evaluate all these learning samples. A teacher must develop rubrics for each type of work. The rubrics will include the criteria and expectations of each work. This will never happen because there is no way to categorize learning for statisticians and politicians.

Effectiveness of the curriculum can be measured only by seeing students improve over the academic year. I love the idea of portfolios. Collect writing samples during the school year so the students can see their writing growth throughout the year. At the end of the year you can go back and look at their improvement. Teachers should have short discussions with each student so they can get feedback about their progress. Portfolios are a great tool for measuring progress and should be used in addition to the state assessments. Not all students are good test takers and sometimes (most times) test scores do not give us an accurate picture of what a student knows.

Test scores cannot be the result of what is learned. You can do well on tests and not be able to apply the information to anything else. As we focus more and more on test data to measure outcomes, we miss out on experiences that are really important for interaction and use of material to real-life situations. Yes, math is important to future life endeavors, but when you use it, you are not performing on a test.

Consider that the future might hold project-based learning as a foundation. Measurement would be found in presentations, peer sharing/teaching, debate, interactions with those with contrary projects. Assessment would come from an enhanced depth of knowledge with a great deal of higher-level thinking and presentations that provided a visceral understanding. Through this, the learning platform would be more than facts and figures, plugging components into equations, or a cursory knowledge of the subject – just enough to pass an assessment.

Curriculum + Instruction + Assessment: The Three Keys

As principal, you need to be aware of the relationship between curriculum, instruction, and assessment [**Grease Spot #53**]. Curriculum, instruction, and assessment all come together to help form a foundation for a successful program in each classroom. Information and processes are what a teacher presents. The way a teacher presents the information is the method of instruction. This could be done in a variety of ways. Classroom discussions, dictation, group work, one-on-one experiences. The teacher creates the method in attempting to help their students understand. Assessment is finding out what your students have learned. This can be done through observation, tests, or any other practical method of assessment. The curriculum drives the instruction, and the assessment shows the teacher what was learned or what needs to be addressed again. Sounds like an Education 101 class, but it is something teachers need to hear during their careers as a reminder.

Baseline

Ultimately, the questions of curriculum come down to basic questions of what is worth knowing, what are the essential questions, and how are these integrated into the classroom?

Noted educational scholar and researcher Robert Marzano believes we should not try to cover all the standards (I am not sure I have ever been in an environment with that set as a realizable goal), but we should address the needs of our students, teaching deeper (not broader), and guaranteeing that what we teach sticks in the minds of our students. Therefore, while teaching to the test is generally frowned upon in most circles, testing what you teach is a best practice. We are still searching for the best assessment model even after all these years of attempting to refine how best to educate children and young adults. Unfortunately, today the answers must be statistical because people do not trust a teacher's opinion of how well a kid is doing in school. *Why?*

Chapter 7

Dancing with the Teachers' Union President
Always Greasy [Grease Spot #54]

No, *Dancing with the Teachers' Union President* is not the name of a new television show or a featured video clip on YouTube. I have, though, equated the principal's relationship with the president of the teachers' union as a *dance* where each wants to lead and yet there is, as in most relationships, a mutual dependency that makes each realize that there is time when you lead and a time when the other leads. The devil is in the details of when and how each segment is skillfully accomplished.

Let the Music Begin

We first must respectfully exclude all of those imperialistic or benevolent dictators, both principal and union president, who practice strong-armed tactics and believe that is the only way to build success. That makes as much sense to me as the term *jumbo shrimp*. It has been my experience that neither person practicing bullying tactics over the other can produce the best results. Please allow me one additional caveat as I set this stage. I am not referring to the contract negotiations segment of the union and administration relationship. The contract negotiations process is so emotionally charged and adversarial in nature that it should remain outside the parameters of the day-to-day relationship between teachers' union president and building principal.

Of significant importance is for each person to understand the role of the other. Because it is within that clarity that one can agree to disagree and do so with mutual respect based upon the recognized and understood role of the other. The primary function of the principal as one initiates the *dance* is to read, understand, and fully bring the teachers' contract into the mechanism of the school. Whether you agree or disagree, like or dislike any or all of the articles, sections, or specific language in the contract, you *must* live by the existing contract and coordinated your school accordingly.

There are two primary functions of the president of the teachers' union: (a) making sure that the contract language (and the word *language* is extremely important, but more on that later) is not violated, and (b) that each teacher has been given fair, due process in any endeavor taken against him or her. It is not the role of the union president to make judgments either about the ability of a teacher to teach or on your decision, for example, to not offer a teacher continuation of employment. However, what a good union president will do will be to hold your feet to the fire to see that all manner of due process for that member of their union has been carried out prior to a non-continuation decision. In terms of any potential disciplinary actions, the same due process component is foundational to the process. Therefore, one of your chief responsibilities must be the prolongation of complete and sufficient documentation.

Documentation

Part of the dance will be the knowledge and understanding that the union president has of your ability to maintain unambiguous, efficient, reliable, and purposeful documentation. These forms of documentation can be as simple as the meeting dates noted on your office calendar, notes of conversations with teachers on an issue that appears to be heading toward a union action, letters and/or memos sent to a teacher about either an area of concern or specific requirements and/or parameters within the teachers' area of responsibilities (and, of course, falling within the scope of their contractual obligation). These one-on-one meetings or formal correspondence are those usually reserved when a teacher has not performed well or up to any aspect of their contractual responsibilities and usually follows at least one oral, informal reminder. The only caveat that I would offer is if a teacher, by his or her actions or lack thereof, placed a student in serious jeopardy.

I would suggest staying away from the use of email as a method of dispensing or for the exchange of correspondence between teacher and principal and principal and union president for potential serious matters. I realize we are in the 21st century, but when it comes to documentation, you need a concrete paper trail of your efforts.

A union president who knows from experience that he or she is dealing with a principal, who maintains well-organized and competent records, tends to address an issue with less bravado and more care. I am not suggesting a degree of paranoia that requires the noting or recording of every event, but you do not want to be caught short without a recorded trail of events and what you did. There may come a time when an adjudicator will want to see an objective trail of events. And even if a situation does not reach the grievance stage, remember many times the district superintendent (and, subsequently, your board of education) will review the issues and your paper trail will speak volumes toward your leadership and professionalism.

The Grievance Procedure

The grievance procedure is another area where your understanding of the mindset of a union will be important. In most cases, a grievance may be filed if you violate the *language* of the contract. Many times, the call is clear: you did A, and the CBA (Collective Bargaining Agreement) called for you to do B. There is, however, the issue of *language* versus the *interpreted intent* of the article or section of the contract and that is where the issue becomes interesting and potentially wire greasing. It is the *interpretation* of what is meant by the contract *language* that many times leads to the grievance. Again, clearly archived documentation of your actions will, at least, pinpoint what you did.

During my first three years as principal, I had eight grievances filed against me by the teachers' union (not a misprint – it was *eight*). I walked into a building that housed three members of the union's executive board and they were pretty much used to getting their way. To give you an idea of how the *us versus them* mentality was, I had one grievance filed against me because I did not approve a teacher's request to attend a conference. This would have been the teacher's thirteenth day out of the building for a conference during the school year! I just thought thirteen days out of school for conferences was excessive. I have to admit I was intimidated by her, she was one of the members of the union's executive board, but I did draw a line and thirteen was the number (although the line should have been sooner than thirteen but, heck, I was chicken).

The teacher filed a grievance because I would not approve the conference for her. Now, this is where is gets a little crazy. This was the fifth grievance filed against me in two years and I was nervous about that many grievances filed against me. I approached the teacher after she filed and indicated that I thought she was a great teacher (I lied; she was not) and that the kids really needed her in the classroom (I lied; they did not) and that there would certainly be more conferences next year but thirteen was a lot of days to be out of class. I will give you thirty seconds to think of what she did next.

You are correct if you thought she filed *another grievance* against me. This time it was for harassment, claiming I was trying to force her to withdraw the original grievance! This was what I was up against. Another teacher filed a grievance because I moved her to a different classroom! I had another teacher file one because I counted the time from the opening bell of school until her first physical education class was scheduled (twenrty-five minutes after the pledge and announcements) as preparation time. Her claim was that because she was not assigned a class or a hall duty, that it was "her" time until her first class started, that it should not be counted as her preparation time because her day did not *officially* start until her first class.

Now, you may ask, why did the union even bother to support these seemingly fluff grievances? Because, as dues paying members, any member who feels aggrieved has the right to grieve, and if the union does not support its dues paying members, the union itself could be sued by the member. The woman whose room was changed and insisted on a grievance indicated that she would sue the union if it did not represent her.

It can also be the philosophy of a union to file grievances to try to expand their contract parameters outside of the negotiation process. Win a grievance, and a contract is expanded based upon the ruling; lose the grievance, and it becomes no harm no foul (you have at least what you had prior to the grievance with an added caveat that no redress will be taken against the grievant and/or the union for filing the grievance).

Please do not get the idea that you are going into a new building and heading into fights with a collective bargaining agency. That is not healthful for you nor is it helpful. I entered at a time when the union wanted to flex its collective muscle, and I had a superintendent who, at the time, wanted to flex back - and I was in the middle! I never made a move sans my superintendent knowing and approving. I suggest you also keep your superintendent well informed of union issues as they rear their heads. And, by the way, if you're keeping count, *I prevailed in all eight grievances!*

In most schools, there are two faculties. One is the faculty represented by the teachers' union, and the other is the one when they are not so represented, and who you work with daily. It is the same people, but it depends on the day and, most importantly, the issue. As a principal, you will need to respect and live by the teachers' contract and respect and take seriously any and all disagreements with someone, or a group, that might have anything to do with living by the tenets of that contract.

On the other hand, contracts meant to protect can also be limiting. You may only do this between this time and that time and only on these certain days but no more than these times per week. If the people trying to find a cure for cancer worked under contract, or to the contract, it will take even longer than it has already.

And the Band Plays On

So what is the best way to *dance*, especially when you could be interpreting the music differently? As with any professional you are working with, honesty builds trust, and trust is the foundation of a strong working relationship. If you are the new principal on the block, meet with the union president to at least establish a face-to-face knowledge of each other. If you are a fixture in the district, and a new teachers' union president is elected, extend a welcoming hand and arrange a meeting with him or her to commence a working knowledge of each other. Don't let your first meeting be one based upon a pressing need.

Remember, in many ways, it is nothing personal. The teachers' union is not attacking you; it is working for its membership. If the union can protect its weakest teacher, then it simultaneously is protecting all of its teachers. If the union can make gains by filing grievances; it will do so. Read and fully understand and comply with the contract. If there is a difference in the interpretation of what can be done according to who is reading the contract, then respectfully agree to disagree and let an adjudicator address the issue. Having a clear understanding of what the role of the teachers' union president ought to be will assist you in understanding what he or she is trying to accomplish when you the music starts.

Union Power, the White Line of Chalk that Cannot Be Crossed

One cannot over emphasize *union mentality* and how it can turn good people bad. Union mentality is not on display often, but it can be extremely influential. As previously mentioned, a union that protects its weakest teacher is protecting all teachers above that level.

I was once involved in a situation where a teacher was being brought up on charges and a dismissal process was underway. The teacher was making students feel uncomfortable by touch them (not in a sexual manner) but simply touching their back, shoulder and/or arm. The teacher insisted that this was part of their pedagogical practice (this was not a classroom teacher but a special area teacher who might have to adjust an arm, shoulder, or posture in order to appropriately instruct). However, the issue was that in the process of performing the act of teaching, students were being made to feel uneasy and uncomfortable and eventually four students complained to their classroom teacher. That teacher subsequently came to me with the issue. During a period of months (the original report came to me in late September) the teacher was spoken with and directly *told* to stop touching students in any manner and for any reason.

The teacher insisted that the learning curve for students would drastically nosedive if proper methodologies were not followed. I informed the teacher I was less concerned about results than I was with the concept of not making kids feel uncomfortable. After weeks of conversations and directives, the teacher continued in the practice of placing hands on shoulders, arms, and the backs of students.

As a result of my oral and written directives (as well as from the department chairperson) and the teacher's consistent disregard for those directives, an insubordination charge were filed against the teacher. Please note that this was not a unilateral decision on my part and that the superintendent was involved with this issue since its outset.

The attorney for the school district and I represented the district and the teacher had an attorney furnished by the teachers' union at the hearing. In my deposition, I noted how I had first heard about the situation naming the students and the teacher who first informed me about the situation. As the hearing began, with an adjudicator sitting in judgment, the teacher who I noted as initially telling me was called to testify. The attorney for the defendant left the room to get the teacher. As the door opened the union attorney returned with the testifying teacher, the teacher abruptly stopped in the doorway upon seeing me and stepped back. The door closed and a few minutes later the union attorney came in and asked for a private sidebar with the adjudicator. I was asked to leave the room so the two attorneys and the judge could talk.

When I was called back into the room, the proceeding went back on the record and a motion was made by the union attorney to have me removed from the room during the testimony of the witness. The adjudicator heard the argument that the teacher would be "uncomfortable" testifying with their principal in the room. The motion was denied by the adjudicator and the hearing proceeded with the witness subsequently testifying that she had never told me about the girls and their comments about the teacher and that she had no idea who the girls were.

The union had convinced her that had she told what really occurred that she would cause a colleague to lose their teaching license and be out of a job, forever. This is an example of the potential power of a union on teachers.

Over Steering, Riding the Clutch and Other Things that Go "Bump" in the Middle of Recess.
Sheepeople

One greasy caution [**Grease Spot #55**] to' watch out for is micro-managing. What if I was out of the building and something need to be decided? What if I was out for the day, a week on jury duty, or longer? During my absence, I want school personnel to be as effective and the school as functional an operation as if I were there. Delegating responsibility for de-cisions is an important part of your managerial function. You will need a clear chain of command. Making people aware of why certain things are done and in a certain manner is a key managerial function in assisting them to make future decisions sans your presence. Knowing why something needs to be performed in a certain manner is as important as knowing what to do. I have one colleague who would receive calls when out of the building asking if the kids could go outside for recess. Recess aides should be able to make that decision. It doesn't require a management directive.

I want the nuances of the building, as well as the school day routines to continue in my absence. If you set yourself up as the *gatekeeper* or the *keeper-of-the-keys* for *all* questions, big and small (remember, Thick and Thin), then purchase a heavy duty chain with a lock and key, lock yourself to your school, and swallow the key. If you do not efficiently delegate, you are not going anywhere or getting much accomplished except responding to the barrage of small, almost insignificant questions that will come at you from everyone. If you have not delegated responsibility, you have not created leaders. You will simply have a flock of *sheepeople*.

As simply as I can put it, there are just not enough hours in the day for any building principal, with a reasonably sized school, to control everything, all the time. Accept it. Get used to it, and then - get over it! If you want to be successful (and my definition of *success* is a balanced work and home life), you had better learn to delegate. Take the time to hire great personnel. Not only great teachers but great secretaries! Great assistants! Great custodians! Great cleaners and maintenance people! Great kitchen workers. Great monitors! Great classroom aides! Whenever you are given the ability to hire someone for *any* position - because in your well-functioning organization there are no menial jobs - hire with gusto, with enthusiasm, and with a focus that Sherlock Holmes would be proud of.

For every minute you spend reading resumes and interviewing, every minute you spend determining whether this teacher should get a permanent position, you will be *paid back* in *years* of smooth operation of the school. Minutes spent on the small stuff gives you years of pleasure and *fewer* problems. Hire great people in and around your office, and give them responsibilities. Yes, the buck stops at your desk and the responsibility of every action and inaction within and around the building ultimately is yours. You are responsible for every student, teacher, non-instructional employee, the curriculum and how well students are learning, lunches, recess, student behavior, student motivation, every brick in the wall, etc., but that doesn't mean you have to make all of the decisions. Hire wisely, delegate, and you will have to make far fewer decisions!

Small Stuff

Some decisions are significant and should be placed right on the lap of the principal. However, there are dozens and dozens of questions that don't require an answer from the building principal. Are the kids going out for recess? Should the band use the band room or the cafeteria for their dress rehearsal? Can Brandon call home because he forgot his homework? May the faculty use the gym after school for an hour of kickboxing workouts every Wednesday? Et cetera!

Trust me, this is not what you want. You want to be out of your office and with the teachers and the students. Delegate responsibilities not as rewards but as the normal part of the job that different people have in your school. In reality, my secretary makes more daily decisions *everyday* than I do.

Initially, you will want to and you must be everywhere and have a hand in everything. That is a normal function of learning about a new school - and about the stakeholders learning about you. The recess aides know the kind of day that I would and wouldn't send the kids outside. My secretary knows when and when not to allow a child to call home. For all of these decisions, I have established a track record and have even made those early, formative decisions in conjunction with those who I ultimately want to make them in the future.

A principal can also not be isolated from peers who have much collective experience as administrators. There is no reason to reinvent the wheel. The first few years as a principal are very overwhelming as one has many irons in the fire. I suggest talking with fellow principals and seeking advice. Also, there are many skilled leaders on every staff and you need to tap into their expertise and empower all staff to share in decision-making. I also believe in making plans. During my first year, I picked three goals and had a sign posted in my office that read, *three things and three things only*. The sign reminded me that I did not have to build Rome in a day and take on everything all at once. I now have a yearly calendar where I list, by month, administrative tasks I would like to complete.

You need to sit back and get a firm grip on where you want to and need to be and, more importantly, where you do not need to be. Sitting in your office or *tied* to an end of a walkie-talkie fielding questions that could be just as easily and just as well responded to by others is not what you want. Are you abdicating responsibility? No. You are using people effectively. It is essential for your success that you use time effectively.

Technology:
Making Sure it is Not the "Third Rail" in the Classroom

Story time, boys and girls! Once upon a time, in a school district far, far away, there was an extraordinary master teacher you would want to teach your child. She has been a master teacher for fifteen years! Children leave her class well prepared for next year and beyond. You never had one complaint about her, and every parent wants their kid in her class. Got the picture? Now, factor in that she hates computers and her Smart Board, never turns them on, and uses them as paper weights or a bulletin board.

Let me toss this out at you and don't throw it back at me too hard! The addition of technology will yield little educational return until school administrators address the need for professional development, technical support, and availability of appropriate software, classroom management, and curriculum integration - in my humble opinion.

Technology Reality Bytes

We are entering the second decade of the 21st century with the expectation of walking into a dark room and flipping on a light switch to illuminate education with the advent and explosion of technology in classrooms. The use of desktops, laptops, tablets, phones, interactive whiteboards and tables, cloud-based learning management solutions, application/software stores, digital textbooks, and the evolving technology ecosystems that encompass all of these hardware and software solutions, signal the new era of education - or does it?

The reality is that our over stimulated student population has been brought up on and seems to require new stimuli every seven to ten seconds to maintain interest and focus. It makes our jobs more difficult because there is a tendency to make us into entertainers. New technology adds to and feeds the *entertainment* aspect of a classroom, and it is the responsibility of administrators to make sure it is equally as educational.

The use of technology by educators in schools is something that must be introduced in a measured fashion and with purpose. There has to be a buy-in and an understanding that the technology will:

1. Provide a useful resource (interactive whiteboards, laptop carts, Tablets, handheld devices).

2. Facilitate communication with parents (email, parent outreach systems, parent portals, and teacher websites).

3. Provide up-to-date information on students, grades, etc. (learning management systems, student management systems, and content management systems).

4. Provide a useful and simple tool to assess students, and/or be able to provide instant analysis for instruction (data mining, RTI, formative assessment tools).

The bottom line is that within the second decade of the 21st century, educators probably should re-think the purpose of technology in schools in terms of the advent of new technology and its exponential growth, access to information, and globalization.

Thirteen Hundred Dollar Drill-and-Practice Machines

Technology in our schools and the potential and subsequent impact on student learning needs to be viewed from the perspective of the classroom teacher and his or her acceptance of, comfort with, and reliability on technology. For without *teacher buy-in* for harnessing the appropriate and effective use of technology, we will end up with $1,300 drill and practice machines, interactive whiteboards that serve as enhanced video projectors, and/or personal Tablets that are $500 notebooks. The issue for any school administrator is not the amount of technology in a school but rather how it is being utilized.

Myths surrounding technology suggest that these tools will make every student smarter and teachers more effective. A multimedia approach to education *may* satisfy this generation of students and their need for constant new stimulation if this approach is adopted by a *skilled practitioner*. Furthermore, we cannot give in to the premise that our school will *look better* if we can proudly boast that every classroom has an interactive whiteboard, multiple computers, and other technology tools. Of late, tablets have captured the public interest. Naturally, schools end up feeling the pressure to equip every student with these hot new devices. However, the issue will always be reduced to these foundational questions:

What are we are doing with the technology that exists in the school?

How do we build upon that foundation in a reasonable, logical, and pedagogically effective manner?

How will the introduction of these technology tools further our efforts to prepare students for the globally connected world so that they can develop the foundational skills necessary for any field or occupation?

A teacher was once overheard responding to the question, "Do you differentiate instruction and please give an example of that differentiation." The teacher proudly responded "yes" to the question and proceeded to illustrate her use of differentiated strategies by saying "if most students get twenty math problems for homework or independent seat work in class, I give some students only ten problems." That was her idea of differentiation. This is tantamount to a teacher indicating her skill with her interactive whiteboard by saying that the kids love to take turns coming up to the board and moving correct answers to the proper location. If a teacher uses an interactive whiteboard like 19th and 20th century classrooms, the board offers no compelling advantage over the chalkboard, pencil, or paper. If a teacher invites students to circle around classroom computers to independently type their answers to a multiple-choice math handout, print them out, and hand them to the teacher, there is no benefit.

Yes, technology is being *used*, but it not acting as a vehicle, in these examples, to further collaborative or investigative spirit. A skilled teacher would invite students to create their own math problems, post them to the class blog, and invite other students to answer them, add comments, post follow-up questions, etc. The interactive whiteboard could be used by students to demonstrate difficult math problems for the class and record tutorial videos (peer-casting) demonstrating the solutions, to be posted to the teacher's website. An incorporation of other Web2.0 tools (wikis, social networks, pod-casting, etc.) could add additional layers to the unit, allowing for communication with other students and schools across the globe.

You Cannot Replace Poor Teachers with Good Technology

Part of the foundational issue is the myopic concept that simply having technology will make us better [**Grease Spot #56**]. The proclamation, "See, we have interactive whiteboards in every fourth grade classroom" means nothing. Either wanting what every other district seems to have and/or not wanting to be the only teacher in the department or grade sans the latest technology tools, *technology-envy* can infiltrate the school mindset rather quickly. Parents may request of principals that their child have a teacher who has an interactive whiteboard in the classroom - as if the interactive whiteboard was the Rosetta Stone or Holy Grail of quality pedagogy. Therein, of course, lies the issue: *having technology versus using technology* properly and effectively. You cannot replace poor-performing teachers with technology, in essence thinking that providing sub-par teachers with technology will make them better or compensate for their ineffectiveness. Poor teachers may become even poorer with the placement of technology into their classrooms.

At best, technology enhances teaching and provides countless new opportunities for students. It is the job of the classroom teacher to organize effective lessons and support those lessons with technology, so as to allow students to intellectually grow - because *technology is an intellectual growth tool*. Technology feeds the intellect because it allows access to information. And therein lies the key to every lesson that a teacher and principal must embrace and understand. In its simplest form, a skilled teacher may first use technology to support pedagogy in the classroom by using it to supplement the educational process. Over time, training teachers to view the use of *technology as an intellectual vehicle* is the proper means to an end and can lead to limitless possibilities, and lessons with depth and breadth not possible without it. Whereas we cannot supply every teacher with a translator, compass, TV station, radio station, recording studio, videoconferencing unit, bus, airplane, spaceship, canvas, set of maps, news reporter, megaphone, etc., we can invest in specific technologies that serve as the *vehicle* or *vessel* to facilitate classroom voyages, conversations, and projects using multimedia tools and asynchronous learning opportunities. In the end, technology can act as translator, compass, TV station, etc., allowing our students endless learning experiences. Teachers who embrace this concept and realize the potential of technology will prepare our students to be communicators, collaborators, and creators of original works. These are the real skills that all students must possess as they move on the workforce.

The Technology Trilogy

We all understand the concept that technology teaches nothing. However, what are the foundational components that will enhance teacher effectiveness with the addition of technology? Educational leaders must look at the *Technology Trilogy* that forms the basis for successful integration. The combination of professional development (good rule of thumb – spend twenty five cents of every dollar spent towards technology on professional development for both teachers and administrators), appropriate software, and technical support.

A systematic approach to professional development will reap the most dividends. The district should look for professional developers who are educators themselves. Sure, an interactive whiteboard company can provide a trainer to show a group of science teachers how to touch the board, use the pens, etc. But, if the company provides a science teacher to demonstrate the different technical traits of the board, while teaching a science lesson at the same time, the group of teachers will likely retain the key *how to* aspects of the interactive whiteboard training session more readily. It is the same concept that effective teachers use in their own classrooms: finding ways to connect the learning to students' own lives.

Once a teacher gets through the anxious first moments of using a new device ("oh no, what if I push the wrong button?"), he or she will recognize over time that the key to successfully using the device in the classroom lies in their software choices. From software packages built specifically for a device (interactive whiteboards, document cameras, etc.), to standard productivity software suites, to new collaborative web-based software subscriptions and open-source options, to curriculum-specific, grade-specific and special education-specific titles, a teacher has many choices. Good professional development units weave in specific software choices that a teacher would use after the training sessions are over.

A symbiotic relationship must exist within the *two layers* of a district technology department: instructional technology and technical support. Once the instructional technology choices are made, professional development is facilitated, and hardware and software are installed, it is vital that the technical support arm of the district technology office supports all the initiatives with a goal of 100% uptime. If a teacher receives a new tech tool, goes for training, and brings back to the classroom the enthusiasm and momentum required to implement the technology in the classroom, the technology tool must work in the environment. Once a teacher gets the sense that there are problems, especially during the early stages of adoption, you risk permanently losing teacher *buy-in*. Of course, there are always *technological hiccups*, so a well-run district helpdesk is mandatory. Teachers should expect prompt responses to technical issues by qualified technicians. Administrators must recognize that good technical support leads to worthwhile instructional technology rewards.

The second concept to keep in mind is that all technology is really doing is allowing for the retrieval, processing, and storage of information. As a principal, you are looking toward enhanced technology as the vehicle toward further and possibly easier curricula integration. Technology is the vehicle for learning new things.

Effective use of technology is not a haphazardly compiled event. It takes time and a research effort to find appropriate information to illustrate an academic point. It takes time to build up a quality instructional strategy that effectively incorporates technology into daily lessons. The fact that teachers are trained to use computers does not necessarily mean that they can use them effectively in their classroom.

The Administrator's Role

There is no question that administrators need to be as well-versed and knowledgeable in the use of technology to enhance instruction as any of our teachers. We must also be in a position to ask teachers those kinds of probing and reflective questions that serve to enhance and build teacher capacity in the use of technology. We must have a clear understanding of what we are expecting from our teachers in the area of the use of technology in the classroom. We need to be clear on how the proper use of technology enhances student learning. In order for that to occur, principals must understand the various components of technology-enhanced learning and how these components are best applied and measured.

It is not enough to do a one shot training session on anything. It is critically important to model, demonstrate, and assist in helping teachers to gain fluency in utilization of these technology tools. Too often technology is mandated and then teachers are left to flounder. This is not good for anyone and something you will have to work against. How can a principal profess that a website can serve to better orchestrate parent communication if the principal is not also using the school website as a communication vehicle?

Web2.0 tools are everywhere. A principal who blogs, podcasts, tweets, or connects with other social tools will likely have the *technological credibility* needed to win the crowd (teachers). You must practice what you preach.

Building Collaborative Technology Teams: The Tech-Teddies, The Bulldog Bytes, The Screen Envisioners, The ESC Keys, The Heads-in-the-Cloud

The seeds of any full and complete utilization of any technology (or even a new curriculum or textbook series) are faculty members who are utilizing (successfully) the new concept. People embrace and learn from people who they can see are modeling the way. The key to success has always been successful sowing those seeds through collaboration.

Creating technology teams either within departments or grade levels goes a long way toward leveling the technology playing field. By utilizing a collaborative approach, the more knowledgeable and skilled teacher in the area of technology *and* pedagogy can work with those who are less skilled at this time and can do so on a collegial basis rather than as an instructor. Letting the *tech-teams* select their own names (*The Tech-teddies, The Bulldog Bytes, The Screen Envisioners, The ESC Keys, The Heads-in-the-Cloud*) serves to drive the camaraderie and start the creative juices flowing. These teams should be approximately six to eight teachers with a coordinator or guide. Teachers formally meet every three weeks and use a shared network drive, a media management solution, or some other cloud-based collaborative workspace.

Lessons, Internet websites and other specific resources are noted and placed into specific lessons and subsequently placed on the network drive. For each lesson good enough to be placed within the collaborative workspace, at least two members of the *tech-team* will use the lesson/activities and present it to their class. This supports two foundational properties:

1. Team members will only share lessons they are proud of. This encourages dedication to build quality lessons.

2. The process of using a lesson a second and/or third time by another educator and with another set of students serves to validate each lesson.

Cooking with the Same Tools

If a chef were training a group of students in a cooking class, he or she would likely provide each of them with the same kitchen tools. Consistency is helpful in breeding similar experiences and allowing for conversations and deliberations about the cooking tasks. Students can talk after class about how they cut certain vegetables and meats, which mixers they used, how long they cooked the sauce on the stove, etc. However, if the chef gave each of them a different set of kitchen tools, the opportunities for shared experiences would be limited, cutting down on the prospects of students helping each other outside of the chef's purview. This same philosophy is helpful from a technology director's perspective, as he or she decides on technology investments. Teachers must receive professional development and will benefit from this time. However, when the training sessions are over, the learning and sharing must continue. *Collegial professional development* is more likely to occur when teachers are using the *same tools*. If three different teachers in a hallway have three different computer models, three different interactive whiteboards, three different document cameras, etc., they will be less likely to share tips and tricks. Stick with the same tools, and your teachers will have many more opportunities to develop over time.

One and Done

A district's commitment to technology is expensive, especially in the initial outlay. The initial costs to purchase and/or lease equipment can be seen by some board of education or community members as "we have met our technology needs by infusing cash and by purchasing hardware, software and other tech tools of the moment, and *we are done*." In reality, this infusing serves as only the beginning. A *one-and-done* technology plan is not a plan but a recipe for disaster. It is vital that a district's technology director act as the lead advocate, building buy-in amongst the principals, district administrators, and of course, teachers. Once buy-in is realized, technology use will go up, and a sustained effort amongst all constituents should follow. This will allow the director the opportunity to present a detailed, sustainable plan to the superintendent and board of education for future technology investments. *If you build it, they will come*, acts as the rallying cry. Once an initial investment is made, it is vital to continue the investment cycle yearly, or the entire technology foundation will crumble, or worse yet, act as an impediment to classroom learning. Outdated technology and the expectation of its use can only lead to wasted time in the classroom and teacher and student frustration. However, when logically approached from a commitment to a plan, the costs are planned for during the span of years including, down the road, the upgrades and/or replacement of the equipment just purchased.

Hit "Send"

The advent of technology in the 21st century signals a new wrinkle in how educators in schools conduct business within our classrooms and the outreach that more liberal and forward thinking people have embraced to utilize the new technology as a means to educate or enhance pedagogy.

Teachers and the educational system will have to retool. The free and seemingly endless availability of information via technology serves to switch the role of teacher from a person with all the information to the person who can open the doors *to* information and, more importantly, who knows how to use the information in a *productive manner* to increase knowledge, understanding, and the *productive use* of the information. Passive student learning, where it has never been acceptable, desirable, or *productive* now becomes the horse and buggy system of learning. Students passively sitting and waiting for information to be loaded into them will fail miserably in the 21st century because they will be missing the skills to succeed. And that is where we as educators must come to grips with how we teach. Passive learning is obsolete learning! It is same as a teacher asking John to pass out the quill, ink bottle and parchment prior to the start of the lesson!

I know I have jumped all over the parking lot in terms of supporting and then not supporting the use of technology in classrooms and by teachers. This is just my little way of getting you to see into every corner of the room, as any good educational leader needs to do. I want students to learn *how to learn new things* in a wide range of areas that lead them into becoming an integral part of the adult society. Learning never stops, and having the ability to learn something new is what helps us to survive through the ages. Technology can be and is a significant key to that lock.

The seeds of any full and complete utilization of any technology (or even a new curriculum or textbook series) are faculty members who are utilizing (successfully) the new concept. People embrace and learn from people who they can see are modeling the way. The key to success has always been successful sowing those seeds. Want to guess what would happen if textbooks for a course were only available online? Would that jump-start tech in a building or what!!!!!

I heard Alan November (the technology education in schools guru) speak years ago. What he said did not hit home to me because my district was doing the opposite of what he said but as the years have gone by I believe he was correct all along. He said that the best use of computer money was not in purchasing computers for fancy computer labs and/or X number of computers in each classroom. He said if you want computers to have a real lasting impact on how kids learn use your money to purchase a laptop for each kid. Fourteen years ago I did not believe him and today he is as right as rain (in my book, literally I mean *in my book*).

It signals to me a new wrinkle in how we conduct the business within our classrooms and the outreach that more liberal and forward-thinking people have embraced to use the new technology as a means to educate or better still to enhance the means (pedagogy). We can get too hung up counting the number of technology units we have in our schools as if they were some measure of excellence. The numbers do not count. It is how we utilize the technology. It is less about what we have as much as it is how we use what we have.

The educational landscape is *instant access* to just about everything imaginable. In part, our job will be to assist students in sifting through and culling the real, the factual, the proven and the useful. How will you, as principal, serve to support classroom teachers and classroom endeavors? What should your classrooms look like? We probably should re-think the purpose of school in terms of new technology, access to information, and globalization. For instance, twenty five years from now, what will a school library look like? Will there even be a library? Or, will you have to see one in the Smithsonian?

School Law

A great change we are witnessing in school law is that more and more individual rights are being accorded to students now than before following Hazelwood, Tinker, and other cases in the mid-to-late eighties. Before individual rights' cases, administrators could make rules and demands that today would be considered restrictive of individual rights. Today, administrators need to be much more careful than they have been, historically.

Next time you get a chance, have a chat with one of your administrative colleagues and ask them about how far out of their thought process, on just about any issues raised in the school, is the *legal ramifications* of what they are about to do [**Grease Spot #57**]. Most administrators are concerned about new laws and their impact that law has upon education (in the classroom and outside of the classroom - administrative law). You would be amazed at the number of times during a day and, most certainly during a *normal* week that I have to think about the *legal impact* of what I am doing and/or not doing.

Law 101

Just a quick and greasy step into School Law 101 and these are basics you will need to be aware of as a principal. Federal, state, and local governments play roles in the operation of schools and the formulation of policy and law. The federal government, through the department of education, administers the public education system. The states have the responsibility for the actual operation of the public schools but the feds are more and more sticking their noses (and the promise of funding – a.k.a., money) into the mix.

The state constitution allows that the state is responsible for providing education. Differences from state to state are a function of the language of the constitution and the provisions, which address educational officials, members of school boards, selection of superintendents and local taxation, to name a few. Similar to the federal system, states have a provision for due process and equal protection of the law. State statues are a significant source of law for educators and they provide principals with specific direction. Case law provides valuable information to principals in the absence of statutes, although a decision in one state is not binding in another.

Locally, schools and principals adhere to policies and regulations of the local school board and their individual schools. School districts are under the control of state and local governments. The school board members are voted in by popular vote, and this board appoints the superintendent, like a chief executive officer of a corporation, who deals with the day–to–day decisions and implementation of policies. The federal government seems to increase control over education (Race To The Top, IDEA, No Child Left Behind, Response to Intervention, Title programs, Common Core Standards) as the federal funding (the carrot and the stick) increases. This is a trend of centralized education. As a result, we may eventually encounter nation-wide, subject-specific, learning standards.

What appears to be heading down the track like a runaway locomotive is that with so many drastic cuts in education budgets, states and schools will be at the mercy of federal funding just to carry out their day to day activities. For better or for worse, any new national assessments will be accompanying the federal funds your school receives. No surprise and a lot of grease, the federal government uses funding to push its agenda.

Rikki Don't Lose That Number

It seems that every child is sent to school today with a lunch, books, pens, pencils, cell phone, paper and the name and phone number of their parent's attorney [**Grease Spot #58**]. I *firmly* believe that a student has *only* two (2) rights when they enter my school: the right to an uninterrupted education and the right to be safe.

I will do anything necessary to uphold both rights, and any student and his/her lawyer can sue me later if you are doing something to keep either of those two things from happening for others and I am taking action to prevent you from doing so.

Biorhythms and Stages

I have this theory about life. It touches on and borrows from the Yin and Yang as well as the biorhythm concepts and I view them through my own (somewhat myopic) lens. For example, if I almost get into a second car accident within a short period of time that I am driving, I believe that I am in a bad biorhythm. I will pull off to the side of the road, slowly count to ten and then drive on. *I want to take myself out of that more negative rhythm.* I also subscribe to the concept that at different times in your life, you are also in different psychological and emotional places (stages).

As a human being you need to recognize that different people working with you are at different life stages. There needs to be a certain degree of tolerance for these rhythms (stages) that people go through. You may, from time to time, have colleagues going through a divorce, the loss of a spouse, a serious illness, or a dependency issue.

You need to adhere to the letter of the contract in terms of employment, and that can be the hard part, especially if a colleague is hurting badly. Just understand and realize that not everyone will at the top of their game every year (and that includes *you*, my friend). There will be times when you will need to support people when they are having a difficult time. There are too many variables to indicate what you should or should not do, but remember that we all go through some tough times and your support of those around you is critically important; professionally and personally. People respect that you need to carry out your administrative responsibilities and they also will respect your understanding, support, empathy and sympathy. As a principal, do not misplace your *human* component [**Grease Spot #59**].

Model What You Expect from Others

I have seen too many people who get anointed with the mantle of authority/power and become unglued (so to speak) with what ultimately becomes *an abuse of power*. You really need to keep that kind of grease off of your high-wire [**Grease Spot #60**]. Speak to people the way you would like to be spoken to and listen to people to a point that they know that you have heard them. (Really hearing and doing what people want you to do are two different things). I play a little mental game with myself when someone stops me in the hallway or classroom. I mentally take off my *principal hat* and put on my *colleague hat*.

There is no doubt that the principal is the center of attention. You will be *modeling the way* with everything you do and say. You will always be *on* stage. It is important not to forget that - *ever!*

Working with your Superintendent

Hands down, the most difficult job in education, outside a classroom teacher, is that of the school superintendent. As a principal, your understanding of what influences and comes to land on your superintendent's desk will assist you to plot a course of action when dealing (working, no dealing) with him or her. While you as a principal have many spokes coming into you as a hub of your building; in essence, the superintendent has but one spoke - and sometimes it is a sharp one - that of the board of education. Yes, there are community groups and other semi-influential community groups as well as district-wide groups that wish to have an influence with the superintendent (and, therefore, the school district), it nevertheless boils down to the board of education that determines the survival of the superintendent. In many ways, it really is a survival atmosphere, and you can affect that survival in a positive as well as a negative way.

In states that do not offer tenure to the superintendent and very few do, the superintendent serves at the *whim* of the board of education. His or her *sole* purpose is to advise and, subsequently, implement the directions of the board in terms of their vision for their school district. The superintendent is hired and stays as long as he or she can carry out the board's mission and muster up a majority vote of confidence from the board of education members. Members of the board of education can and usually do change annually. New board of education members bring new ideas, goals, directions and feelings about the manner in which the current Board has worked and feelings about their chief emissary - the superintendent. They may also bring an idea of who should *no longer* be the district's superintendent. With the potential of a superintendent here today and gone tomorrow, the superintendency is a high-wire act with the *entire length* of the wire greased.

What you, as a building principal, do and say can have significant impact on your boss, the superintendent of schools. I know I have worn out a spot or two in the office of my district superintendent, as I was called upon the carpet for a few issues during the years. However, I believe that my mission is to educate the children in my school, giving them every opportunity possible. The degree of zealousness with which you approach that creed can, at times, put you, *strangely*, at odds with your superintendent [**Grease Spot #61**]. The superintendent's day-to-day mission, in my opinion, is survival cleverly concealed under the sheepskin of *I am here for the kids.* Certainly, having tenure can boost the degree of zealousness of any principal, but I have found it is better to work with your superintendent than be at odds with him or her. Part of that philosophy is that he or she will probably not be around long enough to really influence anything one way or the other.

Reality

Don't be misled by a sweet-talking orator whose pedagogical prose is the stuff that dissertations are made of. The bottom line for each and every super-intendent is survival, and please do not get in their way. So a reality check of where your superintendent is coming from each and *every* time you interact with him or her can place things in the proper perspective and help you to maintain a clean high-wire. I am also convinced that you have some *juice* with your superintendent based upon a number of factors. You can be a new principal or someone that has proven loyal during the years. In both cases, your threat to him or her is diminished, although as a new principal, it is clear where your loyalties lie. However, you will need to be highly effective and make the person who hired you (your superintendent) look good for doing so.

You can and probably should push the envelope a little with your superintendent to ensure the best interests of your students. Let's face it, you cannot and must not be intimidated by your superintendent. There will be times when, if you do not speak up, you may not receive all that should be coming to your school. No one in education gives away money to a school just because you are a great principal. Within your system, the coffer only has a certain number of shekels. At budget time, you will need to be strong and convincing with data and material to support your fiscal requests and in the determined manner in which you ask for what you need. *Determined* is not belligerent. It is also not demanding. Look it up in the dictionary.

You will need to develop *juice* based upon what you can deliver to your superintendent. If your school is quiet and effective, whose parents vote budgets through without much comment you might have a hard time finding some *additional* funding. You will be, for lack of better words, taken for granted. However, with a demanding and strong-willed PTA president, the story is a little different. Now couple that with a large school with many votes for the budget and you are now well on your way to becoming that 800-pound gorilla who can sit wherever it wants to sit - *juice*.

Ugly

Now please go back a few pages and reread Integrity, Credibility, and Trust. I wrote about maintaining your own *Integrity, Credibility, and Trust* in the eyes of those you supervise and the value of the cleanliness of your own personal and professional high-wire. Another perspective is to also view these qualities upwardly in the organizational chain. It might be educational for you, as a leader, to know what it feels like to look at people who have lost their *Integrity, Credibility, and Trust* in your eyes. In this way, it might keep you from losing yours.

A disgruntled parent once wrote a letter to my superintendent complaining in an extremely harsh manner of their displeasure with a disciplinary consequence I provided for their child. The child had committed a *significant act* against our code of conduct. The act was witnessed by an adult and the facts clearly spoke for themselves. However, in an attempt to deflect the focus and take some of the blame from their child – the parent came out swinging (figuratively) at me. Discredit me and you cast aspersions on my decision about their child's guilt and, therefore, the subsequent consequence. The parent wrote a scathing letter about me to the superintendent. The superintendent shared the letter with me. I wanted to write a rebuttal, but the superintendent said that *it would not be necessary* and that *the letter was going to be ripped up and discarded.* I left the office satisfied that I was being supported by my superintendent in the decision that I made about the consequence of the child's action and in the outreach by the parent to the superintendent.

A couple of months elapsed and I found myself walking down a hallway in school and saw a board of education member walking in my direction. We stopped and exchanged a few pleasantries. At that point the board member asked me about *the* incident with the child and the subsequent consequence. The board member's position, as it appeared to me, was strangely leaning toward what I interpreted as the child's/parent's side. I started an explanation and the board member stopped me and said, *"...but it says here in this letter..."*

So I Picked Myself Up Off the Floor

The board member was referring to the letter that my superintendent <u>told me was going to be destroyed</u>! Apparently, the parent who wrote the letter to the superintendent (it was not cc'd to the board of education) was not happy with the superintendent's reply (I was not privy to that conversation or information about the superintendent's reply to the parent). The parent called a board of education member and upon the request of the full board, the superintendent was asked to give them a copy of the letter.

I have absolutely no issue with the superintendent supplying the board with any and all information they want, although that puppy was supposed to be ripped up. However, (think Integrity, Credibility, and Trust) why didn't the superintendent, *at the very least*, inform me that the letter was given to them? Why? Because the superintendent probably never thought for a moment that a board member would say anything to me! The superintendent probably never thought I would find out! *Now, think Integrity, Credibility, and Trust!*

More

Then there was the time that a different superintendent informed *one of my colleagues* that the assistant principal position in my school was going to be cut. The superintendent never spoke to me about it! I was never even asked for my opinion, my feedback or for any input - *nothing!* The superintendent just told an administrative colleague (not a central office colleague but a building level administrative colleague – a peer) to tell me. Now, think *Integrity, Credibility, and Trust!*

More and More

On two separate occasions, I was asked (*told*, in reality) by superintendents to hire a specific teacher who had applied for a teaching position that was available in my school. These were *political appointees* more than anything else even though the full and entire hiring process took place. As a result, two teachers were hired, both with central office and/or board of education links. Now, think *Integrity, Credibility, and Trust!*

These incidents remind me not to treat people with *indifference*. I will re-iterate that the job of a superintendent is not easy and you do not want to get in the way of their survival instinct. I am simply suggesting you lose your *Integrity, Credibility, and Trust* when you do not talk with people. In my eyes, these administrators lost their *Integrity, Credibility, and Trust*. I never felt the same about them again - *ever!* I would **never** want anyone feeling about me the way I feel about them!

Relationships with Fellow High-Wire Performers

I have written about relationships with students, teachers, parents, and central office personnel. You will inevitably also have to establish relationships with fellow principals within the district. Your relationships with these principals are important [**Grease Spot #62**]. At times you will disagree on concepts, theories, goals, directions and probably more than anything else, the methodology to implement the new initiative or to address the perceived need of any issue. Educated people have opinions and administrators are used to making decisions that are rarely second guessed or questioned. How do you collaborate with peers who are also used to being the final word? *Carefully!*

The will be times when the chorus will be unified and singing the same song. However, there will be times when the song will not so sweet and there will be some different opinions. This usually rears its ugly head when joint de-cisions are made that impact a specific building. Here again, *Integrity, Credibility, and Trust* play a huge role.

Example

Long ago and in a school district far, far away, due to budget cuts, building level administrators were sitting around a table meeting as the superintendent's cabinet and responding to the superintendent's request that we come up with an additional $600,000 worth of budget cuts. The superintendent, in front of all the principals, read a long list of all the cuts we had made to date as well as what was still *in* or what had been *added to* the budget for the subsequent school year. Huge cuts like this are never reached by cutting pencils, paper, and textbooks. We are talking people – bodies – employees; and in most cases, that means teachers and/or administrators. In order to reach a major portion of this goal, teachers were going to be cut. At some point during the discussions around the table, I said I would give up my part-time assistant principal to keep classroom teachers from being cut. The cutting of these teachers would subsequently result in higher class sizes. I knew my assistant would not lose his job, just return for a portion of the day to his teaching assignment.

The give-back was graciously accepted and even with a little push-back comment of, *"Are you sure Donald?"* Summing up the meeting, the revisited list was read with the *still ins*, the *add-ins*, and the *new cuts*.

What I did not know and what was *never* mentioned – *ever*, at that table or during the previous half-dozen meetings we had around the same topic (budget cuts) was that in one of the other buildings, an additional portion of time to an existing part-time administrator *was being **added**! I discovered* this by accident a few weeks later! No comments from the superintendent at the table as the long list of ins and outs were read - and, *sadly*, no comment from my principal *colleague* sitting at the table with me as the lists were being read! Please go back and read Chapter 1 on *Integrity, Credibility, and Trust.*

Dealing with Worst-Case Scenarios or Grease that Seemed to Have Been Plopped Down on Your Wire Unexpectedly

Planning for a crisis or disaster seems impossible, and with all the permutations of possibilities, you could easily play the *what-if* game indefinitely. I have always kept three things in mind that are foundation of my crisis intervention plan.

Do you have a plan for the safely of students and staff within your school?

Do you have a plan for the safety of students and staff someplace other than inside your school?

Do you have a plan for the reunification of students with their parents/guardians regardless of where you are? [**Grease Spot #63**]

I have put together a *mobile office* and, in fact, can reunify parents/guardians or other authorized adults with children as efficiently from the baseball field across the street (if we could not stay within our building) or from the fire house or town library if we needed to evacuate the building. I *do not* rely on a computer-based student management system for this purpose but rather good ol' paper! This means that there is a huge suitcase on wheels with a three ringed binder for this purpose. The end result of any issue, catastrophe, or situation will be *where was the principal and how prepared was he or she for this issue, catastrophe, and/or situation?* Your stock raises and/or falls depending upon your actions in a situation that you could never predict would occur.

Hindsight being 20/20, the aftermath and analysis will be tough on you! Be prepared to show your evacuation plans to protect the health and safety of everyone. Whether they worked or not will be the judgment of others, you, at the very least, need to be able to illustrate what procedures were in place. The mere fact that you have procedures will go a long way as opposed to not having procedures and looking quite foolish as Rome is burning down around you. I look at three basic *must be able to do* to cover the multitude of possible issues. All three revolve around safety and knowing where my kids are at all times until each is reunified with their parent or guardian.

1. They are safe in school and need to be reunited with their parent or guardian prior to the normal end of the school day.

2. They are safe on the playing field outside of school and need to be reunited with their parent or guardian prior to the normal end of the school day.

3. They are safe in another location (the fire house) and need to be reunited with their parent or guardian prior to the normal end of the school day.

Have a clear chain of command with outlined responsibilities for the three contingencies I noted above, a clear communications plan, and an evacuation route to a designated *safe* location (ours is the local firehouse three blocks away) will make you look like a genius in the event of an *event*. Make sure that you are *not* the only one who knows the evacuation plans for the school. Between the school secretaries, the clerk in the school library and the three Teachers-in-Charge, the evacuation plans are known by enough back up people.

Near The Last but Certainly Not Anywhere Near the Least

Have the utmost respect for the men and women who maintain the orderliness and smooth functioning of the office - your secretaries. These are the first people most parents, students, and teachers see each day. I let my secretary know where I am going at all times with the only exception being when I need to use the *little principals' room*. It is your responsibility to keep your secretary informed, *well informed*. Your secretary will not be able to be your partner without knowing what is going on – at all times. Provide your secretary with your confidence in him or her. You and your secretary both share fragmented days and this can be extremely frustrating and making it difficult to achieve any sense of completion. Do not forget to say *thank you* often and not just on Secretaries' Day.

The health and, many times, the safety of students are directly in the hands of the custodial crew. You must communicate your priorities for school maintenance to your custodians. Hallways, classrooms, bathrooms, etc., must all be extremely well cleaned – *daily*. Understand their potential frustration of cleaning and cleaning and only having to start all over again the very next day. This can be very frustrating.

Most of these unsung heroes of the school (secretaries and custodians) are poorly compensated, are as professional as any member of any staff, and are equally as dedicated. Relationships with those professionals who are out of the spotlight are equally as important as for those highlighted by it. If you think and act as though custodial and secretarial personnel are not a prominent part of your team then you have a massive amount of grease just dripping off of your high-wire [**Grease Spot #64**].

The Board of Education

One of the more illogical components in the educational process is the ultimate power of local boards of education (BOE). Imagine, if you will for just a moment, a company that is fully *governed* by a group of people who have little or no knowledge of what is the best way to produce the product. They may have used the product, or in this case, board members have gone to school and could possibly have children who either attend or did attend school; but that is it. For the most part, they have no education degree, never taught in or administered a school, and few have any financial background to support their understanding of budgets and related fiscal responsibilities.

They don't need any special credentials. Anyone who is a citizen, a resident of the community and is over 18 years of age can run for and win a seat on a board of education just by getting one more vote than the other person running for that same board seat. Their power is basically unlimited by the state and rarely held-in-check by the constituents of the community. Having written this, the vast majority of board of education members are *wonderful* people who have an altruistic sense of service to the community where they live albeit no knowledge of quality pedagogy or educational practice.

There is no question that because local revenues must be raised and budgets for spending established, that those who *pay-the-freight* should have a say in how money is spent. Local control of education is a foundational constitutional tenet upon which our system is based, however, each of us are probably more than familiar with situations where an out-of-control board of education has disenfranchised teachers and administrators as well as large portions of the community.

It would seem to me that *educators* who live (not work) in the community should have a position on *any* board of education. They can still be elected and run on platforms but their presence should be mandated along with lay people serving as members.

Relationships with BOE Members

Your relationship with members of your board of education is yet another place where, for the most part, you control where and the amount of grease on the high-wire [**Grease Spot #65**]. In most situations, you will have little to do with the board of education other than the occasional Kodak moment and/or to recognize their presence at special events within your school - and this is how it should be. Your involvement in any *political issue* involving the BOE will be an eventual *no-win* situation for you. Stay clear! Stay away! Stay safe! That is why your superintendent makes more cash than you do and that is why you will be in your position years and years after that superintendent has been fired.

While there are certainly boards of education that have the vision and the self-control to establish themselves as arbiters of what would be best for the children in their community, there are others who use the position as a bull-pulpit. Legally, a board of education as an entity (individual members have no authority as individuals – only when they sit in public and make decisions as a total board are their actions legal) have many legal parameters but few moral ones. Too many single-issue candidates run for seats on the BOE, win, and begin to bring to the forefront their specific issues in hopes of gaining a majority of support from fellow BOE members. There are other BOE members who open their email and phones to anyone who has a complaint. Rather than turning that over to the superintendent, *they investigate* (whatever that means). This causes a dizzying array of crossed lines and information overload. A district is then turned upside down. It seems illogical that one person could have so much power but there is a *code-of-boardsmanship* where members will back each other's *pet* projects. And *you* really do not want to become some board member's *pet* project!

You will, at numerous times in your career, deal (work with) all sorts of in-dividuals from the BOE. Most will be pleasant and a mutual respect will be forthcoming as you are seen as a respected educator whose opinion is sort after by the BOE. Many times, the best BOE member is the one that you never see. Members should not be individually wandering the hallways of your school, having meetings with teachers, custodians, cafeteria works, or even with you. That is not their place - now try and stop them - you will not be able to and don't even try; *ever!*

How can you say "no" if a board member wants to speak with you? How can you say "no" if they seek your counsel? Find a way! If not, you will need to measure everything you say. Talk about a grease spot on the high-wire! You really don't want your superintendent thinking individual board of education members are coming to you for information. Forget about the grease; just take a Swan Dive right off the high-wire.

You will need to bounce over this grease spot without losing your balance. A board of education member must have his or her ego well intact and in-check and be aware of their position and their power. The bottom line is that most BOE members feel that they can do anything that they would like to do and most can and will get away with it. Most superintendents will not stand up to board members even though most will try and reinforce appropriate board behaviors. Districts with weak a superintendent have boards that feel that they are mandated to micromanage the district, in the absence of strong leadership. Ironically, in many cases, it is the board's desire for power that handcuffs the superintendent thus causing what the board views as a lack of leadership causing them to rush to the rescue. They have created the very situation they are rushing in to address.

Remember that to serve on a local board the only requirement is that you live in the community and are 18 years of age. From that point on, it's you and how many other board votes you can get to muster them to your *cause*. Do you hate the superintendent because he or she didn't support your effort to get your son on the high school football team even though he was cut during try-outs? Do you dislike the principal because you didn't like the teacher that your child received? Were you unhappy because the budget was increased too high or you feel the teachers or administrators are making too much money? Are you unhappy because your niece was not hired for a position in the school district? Run for the board, get elected, and you are well on your way to sweet revenge.

In addition, nepotism and patronage run rampant in most school districts. It is a good place to be if you want to get your daughter, son, wife, husband, nephew, cousin, or any other person who is living in the house next to you a job in the district. As noted previously, there have been at least two teachers in my school who have gotten their jobs because of board of education/Central Office connections. I accepted the situation and moved on. *Don't spit into the wind!*

Ostrich Administration: The Quickest Way to a Slippery Wire [Grease Spot #66].

It is a rare day during the year when any superintendent I have *ever* worked for just stopped over to the school to see how the kids were doing. So much for, "I am here for the kids." This leads me to the concept of *Ostrich*

Administration; a practice utilized by superintendents *and* a few principals as well.

There is a major phenomenon that sweeps around many administrators and while I find it most prevalent in central office administration, it can be found anywhere. The basic concept is simply *if I don't see it or don't hear about it, I don't know it is happening* (and subsequently, cannot be blamed for it). This is reminiscent of an ostrich sticking its head in the sand to avoid a situation. One can be lulled into the thought that all is well if I am not told or if I don't see anything different.

As an ostrich sticks its head into the sand to avoid a situation it does not want to deal with, *Ostrich Administration* places the administrator in a position of deniability. If administrators are not in building walking the hallways, in classrooms, at bus arrivals and dismissals, in the cafeteria, etc. their head is buried in the sand because the sights and sounds of inefficiency has not reached their ears or eyes.

A lack of *willingness* to see, first-hand, a problem or potential problem prior to rendering a decision is part of Ostrich Administration. I have on many occasions seen central office administration make decisions impacting my school and never having a central office administrator actually seeing, first-hand the potential impact that their decision will have on the school *prior* to making the decision. It seems inconceivable that any administrator would not look prior to leaping but so it is with an ostrich mentality and/or propensity for making decisions in that manner.

As a building level administrator, you will be adding grease [**Grease Spot #67**] to your high-wire by not experiencing, first-hand how your decisions will make a difference - either pro or con. This could be adopting a new textbook series without asking the teachers of the course or making a discipline decision absent input from the classroom teacher.

Administration is not a spectator sport. Nor is it a process that can be successfully accomplished with one's head buried in the sand. You cannot administer from the sidelines. Administrators must be on the field, on the court within the arena of where their decisions will impact. You must belly-up to the place where the impact will be most significant and ask questions, look around, and most importantly listen to the opinions of those who will be in the Splash Zone. This does not mean that they are making final decisions or that you must listen to what they want - but there is a *courtesy issue* and even absent that - even if you are not courteous - there is an *issue of logic*.

The questions of, what if we....., what would happen if....., do you think this might improve.....,; are ones that must be asked. Don't ask those questions, and you might as well be making decisions with your head stuck in the sand!

Example

The assistant principal position assigned to my school, as noted earlier, was eliminated because my superintendent looked at the enrollment numbers and saw a decrease from 774 students to 743 students in one year. The superintendent looked at declining enrollment trends and felt this was the year to eliminate the assistant principal position. I was *never* asked anything, any important questions prior to the decision being *told to me* (by a third party). Never asked how would the responsibilities of the assistant principal be covered? How would this decision impact the students, teachers, parents, the functioning of the school, and oh, yes, me. I surmised that the superintendent was riding in a helicopter over the school one day as kids were entering school and observed thirty-one fewer kids entering the building and made the decision from 1,000 feet above the school. A perfect example of *Ostrich Administration!*

Effective and constructive decisions cannot be made outside of proactive discourse with people - people who will be *splashed* upon.

Chapter 8

Yes, You Don't Need a Bazooka to Kill That Fly.
The Grease of Coming on Too Strong [Grease Spot #68]

Some of the best lessons I ever learned came from those first few months on the job – my first as a principal. And many times lessons learned are from watching others. I remember the first day of school when I was an assistant principal working with an experienced principal who just so happened to be working his first day as principal in this building. I was hired out of the classroom and he was hired from a neighboring district, where he had been principal for eight years.

As we met teacher after teacher during the summer weeks leading up to the start of school, each teacher, independent of the other each, spoke of the need to increase discipline and order within the school. We were asked to bring a sense of discipline and respect back to the building. It became our mantra.

Now, this principal was a great guy with a heart as big as Texas, and he was riding a wave that he believed had gotten him the job in the first place. He had experience in a tough school and had brought discipline to it. He was hearing a mandate from the stakeholders to *clean up Dodge City* – our school. We spent hours listening and even more time developing plans for lunch and recess coverage, staffing in the hallways to monitor students' movement through the hallways, increased teacher supervision in the cafeteria, etc. We developed plans on how the students would enter the building and specific doors that grade levels to enter if students weren't arriving by bus. We moved the bus entrances to another part of the building to better control the flow of students as they came into the school.

Ladies and gentlemen, we worked long and hard and we had *everything* covered. We were ready and bring on the first day of school! We were confident that we would meet and surpass the expectations of everyone. We held a faculty meeting prior to that first morning and presented the *blueprint* to the faculty and staff. The plans were met with tremendous enthusiasm. And

150

so, minutes before the start of the first day of school, my principal and I are standing in the main lobby of the school, side-by-side; Batman and Robin. I had on my polished shoes, a new suit, crisp white shirt, and fresh haircut. I hadn't been so well attired since my Bar Mitzvah. As we stood waiting for the students and parents to enter (this was a K-6 elementary school), we were pumped!

The school bell rang, and through the main lobby door came our kids, as well scrubbed as I was, with their parents in hand. As the throngs started to enter the building, my principal, a tall man with a deep, authoritative voice, pointed at each youngster as he or she entered, asking each child what grade they were in. When they would respond, (I am sure they were expecting a sweet, sensitive recognition of how great that was and welcome back to school) they were met with a stern finger and an accompanying deep voice booming that they should be using that other door because of their grade level and they were told to go back outside and use the correct door! This went on student after student. I remember feeling like a child tugging on my father's coat trying to get his attention. I whispered that we hadn't told them yet which doors to use, so they didn't know. *"They'll learn now,"* he boomed, and he continued with the sorting and assigning of the appropriate entrance door for each child as they entered and noted their grade level. Parents looked shocked, and the first day enthusiasm of the kids was flattened by the principal who was yelling at them - a minute-and-a-half and eight steps into the new school year!

Needless to say, that was not a great beginning for the school year. We had made all these plans. Drawn up all these ideas and created, on paper, a great plan. We neglected one small item. Other than the both of us, no one else knew about the plan. We did not inform anyone. *I assumed* we would visit each classroom that morning to greet everyone and go over a few rules. What a disaster and what a lesson learned! But that was the way he conducted himself, and a year and a half later, he was gone as principal.

What was lost to him was that slow and steady change is the best, and that no matter what the *mandate*, you need to communicate the right information at the right time with *all* the stakeholders.

Who Should Not Become a Principal

While this might be a little too late for some of you reading this book, for those preparing to be a principal, an ounce of reflection is worth a pound of mistakes. I don't think being a principal is inherently difficult (my success is all the proof of that you will ever need) but I sincerely do not believe that it is so easy that just anyone can be successful at it. Ironically, one of the keys to success is longevity. If you last long enough, you'll probably retire from the job – I sound like Yogi Berra.

As time marches on, you will be able to hire your own staff and assuming you do it well, you will start to establish a school filled with dedicated, hard-working, and outstanding teachers. So one might say that *patience* is another quality of a great principal. You must, of course, have a vision of how you would want your school to look and function, but it requires patience to see it to fruition. You need to be around to utilize the patience. You are what you create and a school is always a clear reflection of its principal.

Certain individuals should not become a principal. What types are they? It might be easier to say what they should be like. I believe an effective principal should have little or no ego. He or she should not be enamored by the trappings of power, and they should seek and require little praise. He or she can take a punch or two to their sensibilities and tastes, is pro-child above all else, supports outstanding teachers and those working hard to reach that level, knows how to work a crowd (even a hostile one), and takes *nothing* personally. Someone who can, at times, work alone, someone who believes in themselves and can bring people with diverse ideas at least to consensus. Wearing a red cape, long red leather boots over blue tights with a large S on their chest with the ability to leap tall buildings in a single bounce is strictly optional.

The principalship requires taking risks and possessing the personal quality of being able to lead others. A principal is able to perform skills and delegate in a manner that produces high motivation. A great principal has great enthusiasm. Not everyone can be a principal; it takes understanding, commitment, and a driving force consisting of a high degree of passion (and do not forget your vest that is impervious to those arrows fired in your direction). Principals who put kids first do not look to become or seek to be popular or loved. Principals are goal-oriented people, constantly striving for doing things better. In order to lead, a person must inherently embrace several traits and attitudes: ambition, drive, cognitive ability for analyzing problems, compassion, empathy, honesty, a sense of humor, integrity, sound morals, and ethics.

How Fast Are You Running?

Many of us are so driven in our own personal and professional lives that it is hard for us to remember or even imagine that many people are not as driven. Many people need an outside source of motivation to try harder or do more than *just enough*. It takes a good administrator to bring out the best in his or her staff. It also takes a *careful administrator* who realizes that pushing or driving people too hard can be a greasy spot on that high-wire [**Grease Spot #69**].

Your *juice* that has gotten you this far is not transferable. There will be times when you will be waiting for poky puppies to catch on, catch up and/or catch hold to what, where, when, and how you are heading. Your desire for something to be accomplished, fulfilled, completed, or even started *yesterday* is not the same time commitment that others might have even though everyone around the table agreed to get the same job completed.

How do you motivate the less motivated among us? How do you get someone moving closer to the speed you desire them to move? My suggestion is that you *push with a balloon* (and try not to pop that balloon). You can support, work alongside, remind and prime-the-pump to get someone off of square one or to a point of near completion of a project. However, you cannot push, coax, cajole, intimidate, or, in anyway, force someone to move along faster. This is especially true *if they volunteered to do something*. You will never get someone to volunteer to do anything again in the school if you are seen as someone cracking a whip. Yes, you might get to a point where you must say to yourself, *I selected the wrong person for this job*. You will be wiser next time prior to stepping on that spot on the high-wire.

It also will be seen poorly by others if you whisk the project away from the person and finish it yourself, for now you have embarrassed someone in front of the entire school. Choose your options and activities wisely. A lot of people are watching; in fact, everyone is watching!

Never Let the Day Start Until You Do

All things being equal, I try never to let the activities of the day start before I am ready [**Grease Spot #70**]. While there will be events during the day - a crisis brought about by a student, teacher, parent, or someone from central office that will force me in a direction I had not foreseen - I nonetheless do prepare for the day and attempt to meet and begin the day on my own terms.

I get to school a good hour to an hour and a half prior to the start of the school day. I enter into the school day at my own pace. While the starting time of the school day remains the same, the precursor to the day is mine. You need to be prepared for the day and your pre-school rituals allow you to meet the day on your terms. You need lead-in time, you need to be ready for the day before the first bell, and you need to be 'started' well before it rings.

I control when I visit classrooms, when I walk the halls, when I show up at bus duty, as well as my presence in the cafeteria. I try not to establish a discernible pattern because the fact that I can be at any place at any time is an advantage that will work in my favor. I control when I want to have that parent meeting and when I summon a particular child to my office. I also seek to control when I need ten minutes for myself to take a deep breath, take stock, and try to start and finish my lunch....in peace.

Do not be afraid to let your secretary know you are having lunch and short of blood spewing forth or the president calling - that would be of the United States and not of the board of education (although many times the latter thinks he or she is the former) - that you need some down time. A good secretary will get you not only ten minutes but probably twenty more. Do not be afraid to take the time for your own physical and mental health. Heck, twice a month, get out of school and have lunch with a fellow principal! Need some additional mentoring, email me and take me to lunch!

Never let the day start before you do and never let the day control you! It sounds simple and it can be hard to do on certain days but it is necessary that you strive for this kind of control of your day - or at the very least, the beginning of your day.

Trader Joe's

One of the simplest ways I can put it and one that really hits home for me is the Trader Joe's comparison. Where do you shop for groceries? Pathmark? Shop-Rite? Stop & Shop? Walbaums? Think about the people who serve you in those grocery stores - how they respond to your inquiries, request for assistance, and their unsolicited inquiries of could they help you?

Now think Trader Joe's! If you have never been in Trader Joe's, please find one and go shopping. *I want the school where I am principal to be like Trade Joe's.*

Trader Joe's employees have a special way of greeting people and providing services to their stakeholders (customers). They are friendly, informative, and helpful as well as being extremely knowledgeable about their products. The ethos of the store is created by management and carried through by employees, and it is the expectation that they will work with the people they come into contact with each day.

Certainly, we are dealing with things more significant than a can of corn. We are working with the children of our stakeholders, a far cry from a can of corn. However, it is the Trader Joe's ethos that creates the environment and you should try to create that environment in your school (and they do have the best fresh squeezed OJ on the planet).

Mirror, Mirror on the Wall, Was My Last Decision the Fairest of Them All? [Grease Spot #71]

Absent the ability to utilize and/or having access to a mirror that can foresee if you are, in fact, the fairest of them all; it is important that you have at your disposal the ability and process to professionally develop your skills. As principal, basically everything we do is on-the-job training. Unfortunately, it is imperative that the majority of your decisions are correct; *the first time*. Within that context, the complexity and ambiguity of being a principal necessitates that we reflect on our actions and deeds and the subsequent impact on our stakeholders.

The best scenario for our professional growth would certainly be a peer group process to support and/or challenge existing theories and preconceived views that influence our decision-making procedures. However, the reality of that occurring on a regular basis is rare and frankly, who are you really comfortable enough with to open up to the degree necessary to promote effective and lasting internal change? The mirror to introspection is to develop a *reflective practice* that enhances your capacity to reflect on your professional practices.

Building a Reflective Practice as a Professional Development Strategy to Support Administrative Decision-Making

The importance of reflecting on your decisions is critical for continual and sustained growth. Developing a practice of *critical reflection* based upon experiences and proactive thought processes, can prove to be an effective technique for professional development.

Donald Schon, in 1983, noted reflective practice as a process in refining one's ability. Reflective practice is a way for neophytes and veteran practitioners to build upon successes and learn from failures. As defined by Schon, reflective practice involves thoughtfully considering one's experiences in applying knowledge to practice. Operationally, reflective learning is self-motivated learning. It is a process that requires discipline and focused *critical thinking* about your processes and subsequent interactions with people.

Critically Reflecting on Your Decisions

Gaining an understanding of what a reflective practice is and the process of entering into a continual reflective environment is important for professional growth. The notion of reflection as a contributor to the improvement of practice has its roots in the work of John Dewey. For Dewey, reflective thought (as he referred to it) is provoked by an event in one's life that arouses a state of doubt, perplexity or uncertainty and leads to the individual to search for possible explanations or solutions (1933). We, as professionals, must view our initial understanding of a situation and our actions surrounding that situation and develop an understanding of what led us to generate the solution that we operationalized.

If you buy into the concept that *expertise* comes from *experience*, it is not enough to expect that physical experience alone will lead to a high level of expertise. Within any period of reflection, there will be ambiguity and uncertainty. However, that ambiguity and uncertainty is an important part of the process. Your ability to analyze your own thinking process is a keystone that needs to be honed and cultivated.

As practitioners, it is beneficial to critically reflect on practices, focusing on weaknesses as determined by the outcomes of decisions, and tracking repetition of practices that led to either good or less-than-stellar outcomes. Conceptualizing in this manner allows you to note similarities in your decision-making process and the possible influences, both internal and external, that might have influenced those decisions.

Teaching Yourself to be More Reflective

As you reflect, you need to look at your response process to both familiar and unfamiliar situations. What were the steps used to come to the decision? Upon reflection of the results of your action:

- Did the decision come to a positive fruition or not? Why?

- Would you rethink the deliberation that lead to the decision, if it was a less than satisfactory outcome?

Part of the reflection process is a response to the question; *was a logical deduction process used to ascertain the decision?* Becoming a reflective person is a conscious, deliberate, and systematic process of training yourself in light of consequences of your actions and you must be willing to question your practices in a purposeful manner.

The path toward a solid reflective process is a constructive system of analysis, change, and restructuring. The consequence of the decision, effective or not effective, must be analyzed in terms of what went into your decision-making effort. For example:

- Prior knowledge.
- Attitudes and desires of influential people.
- Prejudice or a particular leaning in a certain direction.
- Did you discount, ignore, or limit input from others?

- Was there an ego-related component added into the decision-making mix?
- Did you think too long or too hard on the issue and became paralyzed?
- Did you not give the issue enough thought and/or lead-in time?
- Did you have enough information to make a good decision?
- Was the impact of the decision more or less than you expected? Why?
- Did people ignore, act complacent, or become agitated as a result of your decision and/or their degree of involvement?

The period of growth, as you respond to these types of questions, commences when you ask yourself; *how, given the need to make a similar decision and/or the next decision; will I/should I react?*

Developing a Critical Distance

You need to create a *critical distance*. It is impossible to judge an event or experience as it is happening, so the aspect of *critical distance* places the administrator, either following the event (with its consequence in full view) or at a more proactive juncture, where the decision has not been finalized because you are in the thinking process.

As an administrator, there is no question that many times a sense of doubt can be a prevalent concept floating in your mind. That sense of doubt can begin to dissipate as you became more and more reflective. The key here is that reflection leads to more reflection. As you get better at the practice, it becomes easier and the pattern that your decision-making takes, and the analysis of the results, becomes clean, crisp and clear.

Serve and Volley

The best metaphor I can suggest is tennis. The majority of shots you drive across the net are reflex actions based upon determining the speed of the ball coming to you and the angle at which you set your rack as the ball hits it. All of these are instantaneous reactions to the ball being hit in your direction. This is not unlike your average day as an administrator with questions and situations coming at you fast, often, and even aggressively. Your experiences will allow you to make the best response you can. However, when you are preparing to receive a serve, you have time to wait, think, anticipate and decide how you are going to move when the ball is eventually hit to you. The knowledge gained from those serve opportunities set up your instantaneous decisions *during* the match. After the game, you reflect on the shots made during the match and how adjustments (body position, racket angle, and speed) could have influenced your volley. This is pure reflection with clear, obvious indicators of whether you prepared and sent the ball where you intended!

Reflecting on Reflection

The self-inquiry system causes you to take a step back and critically reflect not only on how you approached a situation, but also on why you responded in a particular manner. The questions of who was involved in the decision-making process, who was not, who should be added in and who should be deleted, are all part of this dynamic process to gain a deeper understanding of your own administrative style, deliberation process and, ultimately, enhance your effectiveness as a principal.

We tend to shy away from people we see talking to themselves and think that they might be crazy. The bottom line to *productive* professional development utilizing a reflective practice is that you will need to talk to yourself. However, in this case, if you don't, you might be crazy not to take advantage of this strong professional development practice!

Reflection on Professional Practice

Consider some of the ways of reflecting: Beginning the day with reflection of the previous day's activities, problems, and successes allows time to think about these events. Ending the day with reflection that gives you a quick glance at the day's adventures.

Reflection also allows leaders to stop and analyze routines, work flows and the communication that has taken place. Like watching events on instant replay, reflection provides an approach to analyzing different objectives in your school environment. Learning from our experiences is an aspect of leadership that uses reflection as "major ways in which leaders learn from the past" (Bennis, W. 2003, p. 108) and the many experiences, both positive and negative that effect leadership. It is negative events or occurrences that get most of the attention from leaders. It is "unfortunate, too often these people's failures that get them to reflect on their experience" (Bennis, W. 2003, p. 109). You must see reflection as useful in all areas of leadership. Reflecting on the positive is just as important to understand why a certain process was effective and worked as planned.

"When you're going along, and everything is working well, you don't sit down and reflect; which is exactly the moment when you should do it" (Bennis, (2003), p. 109). In leadership, time is everything. But the time leaders spend on reflection is just as vital as the time they spend planning, as reflection is a vital component of planning.

In leadership there are many mistakes that take reflection to the level that most principals use it. Thinking about methods of change that could turn our failures into a success, is a basic step of organizational planning, but not the most important. Leaders need to realize that it is those "mistakes that contained potent lessons - but only if we think them through calmly, see where we went wrong, mentally revise what we're doing, and they act on the revisions" (Bennis, W. 2003, p. 111). Maturity in leadership is the ability to admit something did not work as planned, and then listen to those who completed the task. This is essential to growth as a leader and ultimate, the growth of your school. As a by-product, if teachers see that lessons are learned from failures, then they are more apt to buy into the changes necessary for organizational improvement.

Yesterday's Newspaper

I have always had this idea that the teachers and I are as valuable to the parents as yesterday's newspaper. During the time a parent's child is in a teacher's class and your school, in most cases, the earth revolves around that teacher. After all, who is not to some degree intimidated by their child's teacher or teachers! Parents have a lot *riding on* that teacher or be it a series of middle school or high school teachers or that single elementary teacher's influence for the entire school year.

I equate this to the current day's newspaper being in your hand. That newspaper is important to you, it contains things you want to know, it provides a service, and until you are finished reading it; it is of value. Now, let's think about the value of that paper when you see that same newspaper the next day. Unless you are moving, own a parrot, or you are creating a large papier-mâché' piñata, the value of that newspaper has depreciated, *significantly*.

And the value in the minds of many parents, of their child's teacher after that final day of class for the school year is about the same. So too does the school principal devalue once the child has left the school. The adage of what have you done for me lately could not be more appropriately affixed to this situation. How have I come to this mindset during my professional career? I simply have been looking and listening.

Target

Educators have been targeted by every group of community members who want to rein in spending in their community. I dare say that every parent wants that $100,000.00+ teacher, the one with experience and reputation for excellence. But the same parent will rear up against that teacher's salary as soon as they are finished with him or her. They do not understand the concept that the greater good a community is enhanced by having an outstanding education system and the direct result a quality school district can have on the value of their home.

I have attended board of education meetings where parents applauded the latest speaker who steps up to the microphone and rails against the overpaid and underworked educators and have seen parents I knew were thrilled and extremely satisfied with their child's teachers clapping wildly in support of speaker after speaker denouncing teacher salaries. It is simply a matter of yesterday's newspaper - I am done with you; you are of no use to me any longer.

The issue of disposability has no merit when viewed from the prospect of how an outstanding school system can enhance the property values of the entire community. It is short sighted and counter-productive. I have a hard time understanding why educators are held in such poor regard. It could be possible that many of us do not dress professionally at work. I dare say you would probably not have confidence in a doctor or attorney that dressed the same way some teachers dress - there goes the professional angle.

Or is it as simple as people view us as not working hard enough? Weekends and summers off, not to mention all major holidays. Jealousy? All those parents had the opportunity to become teachers, but back then teachers were grossly underpaid. Believe it or not a decade ago people actually felt sorry for us because of the difficulty of the job and the low wages.

Aesop

What has happened is the oldest of Aesop's Fables - *The Tortoise and the Hare*. Slow and steady, year after year, decade after decade, teachers have pulled in small but steady increases in pay and compounding interest has evolved veteran teachers to over $100K salaries. Add to that significant health insurance coverage and, at least in New York State, a retirement system that is one of the strongest in the nation and guaranteed by the Constitution of the State of New York.

Add all of that together and a two-and-a-half month summer vacation and people are angry with us and see us as the reason for the economic issues or at least one of the reasons that they cannot get out of their economic distress. Accurate? Absolutely not but as school budgets are the only tax increase that can be directly voted on, the school system becomes the easy targets of the over taxed and angry community populations.

If it was up to the taxpayers who have now used their newspaper and see no value for it (us) any longer, all teacher and administrator compensation would be something like the following: We would be taken to a different student's home each week. We would be fed and sheltered there for one week intervals. Medical benefits would be cut to zero, and we would receive medical treatment when we stayed at the home of any doctor or dentist, psychologist, or chiropractor living in our district. All school employees would work 365 days per year, and during the summer months, we would work at the beaches, parks, and do lawn maintenance on the grounds of state facilities.

The solution, easy! I would place every one of those complaining newspaper discarding people in a classroom with twenty-five to thirty kids. I would provide them with the curricula to teach and one hundred and eighty-one days to do it and say "start" and I will see you in ten months! I would subtly add that the career success of all of these kids probably in large part hangs in the balance of their effectiveness - see you in June! Most parents cannot tolerate or handle their own child's birthday party with eight kids for three hours.

Braindroppings

Ego

"There is something of an ego investment in the leadership role for many managers, an investment that presumes leaders are smarter than subordinates and that leaders broker most of the information that is important to the organization" (Marion, 2005, p. 111).

I have a little pillbox in the glove compartment of my car. Every morning as I pull up to school, I open the glove compartment and open the box. Just before leaving the car, I drop my ego into the box. I close the box and put it in the glove compartment, close the glove compartment, and then close and lock the door of the car - tight security for something that if it got out of control could seriously inhibit my high-wire walk [**Grease Spot #72**]! E-g-o can spell self-destruction. Your ability to maintain your role and, subsequently, your effectiveness as a principal over the duration of time involves ego. It is almost impossible to be the principal (just apply the definition of principal) and not have an ego boost. It is how you handle that boost of your ego status that will result in your ability to balance on the high-wire. The perspective of how important you are to the organization and the effectiveness of the school creates ego. The concepts of "I am always right" or "they cannot do this without me", starts you on your inevitable plunge. No school on record has ever *closed* because a great principal left! However, egocentric administrators have caused many a school to reel back from the sheer pollution caused by an out-of-control ego.

Your guide must be your perspective of your role in the organization. No one part is greater than the whole and no one person has all the correct answers. The more correct answers you think you have already signals that you have missed the first question - *what does it take to have an effective school?* A myopic lens can only allow you to see in a limited fashion. What a principal needs to understand is that as more and more accolades flow towards your school, it is increasingly more important to realize that you were not the *only one* to cause this to happen.

The praise received by the principal for a job well done cannot stop in the principal's office. Success of a school is due to a large variety of factors - realize that quickly and when success comes at you be confident enough in yourself to step aside and let the accolades pass onto the others who worked as a TEAM to create the success. You surely paved way and established the course, but everyone was on board and worked hard.

Success

Success can be an ego builder and can be misinterpreted by someone in a leadership position as directly attributed to them. Certainly someone charts the course and has the vision but just as certainly no one person can do everything alone. There is also the ego that creeps up on you. Your school has had a great deal of success and accolades come streaming down. Over a period of time you are buoyed by success and as a leader those accolades come to you. As long as *you*, as the principal, realize that you did not do it alone, you will be on a grease-free high-wire in checking your ego. Or do as I do, check your ego as you walk in the school door each day in the glove compartment - for a word with so few letters (E – G – O) it can create a great deal of grease!

Charisma

If required to describe myself and my personality the thought of a bowl of vanilla ice cream placed upon a radiator in the middle of a January blizzard comes to mind! And so the term charisma and its association with leadership and leaders is a difficult one for me to comprehend. Given my self-description, a charismatic personality is something I am not blessed with. John F. Kennedy was someone whose charisma probably served to propel his leadership style and potential. I will let historians debate his success as a leader but it was un-mistakable that his personal charisma reached out to many. Did that make him a great leader or did it just get him in the door? The question then becomes, *how far can charisma carry you and for how long* [**Grease Spot #73**]?

One's ability to communicate effectively adds to one's charisma and is the first thing that most people notice. But for how long can charisma keep you up on the high-wire? My prediction is not for too long. Personally, I would not worry about having or developing charisma because over the long haul, it plays little into the concept of competency and/or effective leadership.

Miss Congeniality

Popularity is and has *always* been highly overrated. You will not necessarily have less grease upon your high-wire because you are *popular* (why do I sound like I am in high school?). You want to be effective and not necessarily popular. The high-wire path is not a popularity contest and sustaining yourself on the high-wire via popularity will last an incredibly short period of time [**Grease**

Spot #74]. Sustainable results from effectiveness are what counts. It comes down to in your professional endeavors would you rather be *liked* or would you rather be *respected*? At first glance it does appear that effectiveness is related to popularity because being effective is a quality that many people like.

There is a difference between congeniality and collegiality! Your high-wire is straight and clean once you set your course with the thought that you are striving for collegiality at all times and your responses and reactions are always in the collegial ballpark. This is because you will, from time to time, make a decision that just might anger some people. Yes, it is true, it will happen to you as a leader. You should be striving to have your acceptance based upon integrity, credibility, and effectiveness and not popularity. You will be abdicating your ability to grow into an effective leader if it is based upon popularity.

Another self-imposed greasy spot on the high-wire [**Grease Spot #75**] is your inability to have your actions keep pace with your words. Please do not say anything that you do not mean, cannot prove and/or will not or cannot do. If that is how you intend on living your career then leave educational leadership and enter into a profession where those attributes are better suited – *politics*.

From my professional dress to my demonstrated respect for teachers, parents, students, staff members and all other stakeholders; what I ask for I give. I believe it is a true and telling component of who you are in terms of credibility. This is because I stand for and by what I believe in.

Death by Mosquito Bites

If given the option between death by mosquito bites or giving a speech, most people will probably select the former. Public speaking is not usually high on anyone's, *Oh, I love to do that* list. One of your main functions from time to time will be public speaking. You will probably not give too many *formal* speeches, but you will have numerous opportunities to address your faculty and staff as well as your parent teacher organization. I would suggest that you do not take any opportunity to speak in front of people lightly and certainly if called upon to present at a BOE meeting. Failure to plan adequately will make you appear awkward, at best, and will certainly be a grease spot [**Grease Spot #76**] on your high-wire.

One key factor to keep in mind is that passion is contagious. You will need to pass that passion on through your words, your tone, your mannerisms, and your eyes. People will react to your reaction to what you are presenting. Regardless of your audience, a great presentation must be of interest to your audience. Mentally, place yourself in the audience and as you prepare your speech think of what they will be hearing from you and what you want them to know and walk away with from the presentation.

My *strongest* possible recommendation is *do not*, under any circumstances, try to memorize your speech and/or presentation. You are one short senior-moment away from looking very foolish. Someone with notes appears to the audience as someone *very* prepared and *very* professional.

I suggest writing out your speech and placing it on four-by-six inch index cards. The mere transition from one card to the next creates nature breathing and pause spots within your speech. I place a / mark in between words where I want to make a one beat pause, two // marks in between words or sentences where I want a two beat pause, and three /// where I want to make a major point or emphasis. I use a red pen for these /, //, and /// marks, so that they stand out. (Number each card in order just in case you find yourself engaged in a game of 52-card pick-up!) Please do not use eight and a half by eleven sheets of paper as you can easily lose your place and the rustling pages can be distracting.

It is not a bad suggestion to record yourself presenting the speech to pick-up on the idiosyncrasies that might be there and that you are not aware of; such as excessive use of the words "well", "hum", "like", "O.K.", etc. We have all heard people present who have these *anchor words* that permeate a speech and can be distracting. Most times, even your best friend will not tell you that you are doing this for fear of embarrassing you.

I will suggest, with caution, that adding humor to the speech is a very good idea. However, be advised and warned that one person's joke is another person's insult. Stick to generic topics for you joke and/or some degree of self-deprecation.

Giving a speech is a great time to show off your knowledge, your skill, your passion, and your position as a leader. Do not shy away from the opportunity. Embrace the chance and make it your own and a realize it is a great grain of sand on your beach.

How Do You Want to Be Remembered?

One of the fundamental questions that you must ask yourself before you venture out onto the high-wire is, *how do I want to be remembered?* I believe that should be part of your vision for whatever school you have become principal of and is a summative factor as you someday look back and review (your career path) the results of your efforts. While walking the hire-wire of being a principal, you are on a direct and one-dimensional career path and your decisions of where to head takes on a Robert Frost-like setting as paths diverge (on a snowy high-wire).

With all of the possible changes and the vast opportunities that will be available to you as you traverse your career, I think having a clear picture in your mind of what people will be saying about you at your retirement dinner or what they will be feeling about you as you leave the school district should guide your daily practice up to that point. I use the retirement dinner scenario because using the analogy of what people will say about you in your epitaph/eulogy as a light to guide your daily actions is too depressing. And besides, at the retirement dinner, after a few drinks, everyone looks good!

Your mantra should be consistent regardless of where you are a leader. It probably should have a tremendous amount to do with kids and keeping them safe and providing for their enhanced potential for a great education. I would suspect that you would seek clear parameters of what will and will not be tolerated by students, parents, and/or teachers. I think those fundamental concepts far outweigh results. I write this because, in many ways and in many situations, results will be realistically out of your control. Certainly, if you plant yourself in one district long enough to hire all the teachers in your school, you have a chance of creating real change and reaching success.

I am not sure that flash-in-the-pan movement, three to five years in one place and then moving on, can generate enough time to create a *real* difference in the ethos of a school. I would think that your commitment of anywhere between six to ten years is minimum. I am not sure who among the school's stakeholders would follow you if they thought that you wouldn't be there for the long haul. Teachers are trees that take root in the soil of the educational community. Few of them are transplanted from the district that initially hired them. It is only logical then to assume that they want someone as committed to their school as they are, and many people translate commitment to time in the place.

An administrator's career can be one of transition. The fact that you are an administrator almost carries with it that eventual movement. As stable as most teachers are, it is the antithesis for an administrator. The initial inroad, assistant principal to then becoming a principal, most times requires a movement out of district. Some would suggest that you probably wouldn't want to be an administrator in a building where you were a teacher. Others would suggest that it doesn't make the high-wire greasy by staying put but rather makes that wire thicker!

Either way [**Grease Spot #77**], you will need to convince everyone that you are here for the long haul and that commitment will result in positive results for the students of the community.

Now Forget the Grease, Stress is the Body's Rust

Good school management is as important to your success as assisting in the development of curricula and/or the fine tuning of classroom pedagogy and management. For one thing, not having a school that is functioning well can cause you daily stress. Stress is to the human body what rust is to metal [**Grease Spot #78**]. Stress can come from all those around you; central office administrators, the board of education, personal and family life, the community, as well as students, parents and teachers! Just as surely as rust eats away at metal, stress eats away at your body. Stress reduction can be achieved by a logical, reasonable, and comprehensive series of managerial plans for the variety of phases of your responsibility. As noted earlier, just imagine what potential issues can be eradicated with just two, short, five minute meetings; one with your secretary and the other with your head custodian. Now carry that premise to the next set of logical steps for each member of the staff that might benefit from a touch-base with you.

Creating and maintaining a well-functioning, a well-managed school is less about being everywhere at one time and more about making sure that you are in the right place, at the right time and communicating with the right people. The management of relationships for a leader is their ability to influence others to work towards the vision of the school. In summary, I am reminded of the passage noted at the beginning of this book and in De Saint-Exupery's, The Little Prince; "If you want to build a ship, don't herd people together to collect wood and don't be so rigid to assign tasks and work, but rather teach them to long for the immensity of the sea."

Success Secret

Someone, at the conclusion of one of my college classes that I instruct, asked me what were the secrets of my success as a school principal - albeit, who am I to say I am truly successful. After I responded to him, I made it one of my closing remarks to all of my classes. I submit it to you not as an ego boost for me, but I always, even after all these years, still swear by the summary, and each time I think about it, I say, *"Yes, that is it."*

Reading all the books (including this one) about theories and strategies and the lists upon lists of what to do as an educational leader is great brain fodder. But remember in theory communism works - and I could probably find a list of what to do to make it work!

I never taught a day of elementary school except as an art teacher and that was fifth grade art. And yet my elementary school, during my tenure as principal, received both New York State and U.S. Department of Education recognition for its Overall Excellence. I got to meet the President of the United States because of those recognitions and the next year Redbook Magazine indicated that we were one of the 72 best elementary schools in the country. Ten years later, I was recognized as the New York State Elementary School Principal of the Year and, subsequently, a National Distinguished Principal. I was again honored in Washington, D.C. including a second trip to the White House.

So where is my list of things to do to become a successful principal? I have none because it is *my* list that works *for me* and probably would not work for you. Advice? Now that I have a ton of....

Remember who the experts are - the teachers! Remember if you ask them, they will tell you what works for kids. Don't be afraid to grant tenure to *only* the best of the best. Laugh every day, and if you can't laugh find another job. Get to school early and stay late. Be visible in the classrooms, hallways, and cafeteria. Expect twice as much from yourself as you do from others. Treat others ten times better than you treat yourself. When new programs come to your school, attend the workshops *with* your teachers. The final piece of advice is to go back and make sure you do the first three or the rest will not matter.

We are in a people business. Be polite. Be firm. Be respectful. Be demanding. Be visible. Be logical. Be understanding. But always be yourself and see if that works for you. If it doesn't work, well, education is not the only profession. My plumber gets $125 as soon as the front tire of his truck touches my driveway.

Closing

Successful leadership emanates from a variety of *crucial competencies*. These talents include impeccable communication, inspiring vision, healthy emotional intelligence, and strategic thinking and planning. However, this only scratches the surface of the myriad of skills required for a strong and well-balanced principal. A foundational imperative, however, is *personal integrity* that aligns with organizational ethics or standards of conduct. Leadership is based not on ultimate power and authority, but on principles, people skills, and the ability to encourage people to come to consensus about *critical* decisions and solutions to problems.

Thomas Jefferson, my favorite person from history said, *"Good government is less government"*, and I just switch the word government and put in leadership - and it makes all the sense to me and it works for me. I have been able to prove it based upon what the faculty and I have been able to accomplish in over four decades.

What distinguishes a good principal from a great principal is the attained levels of success. Good leaders will be successful, but great leaders will be successful over a sustained period of time. Great leaders *will always* have people who are willing to follow them and their style of leadership, because they know that whatever task that is undertaken by that leader, they will be successful in fulfilling that goal. Great principals know how to map out their journey in order to be successful, they know how they are going to accomplish goals, and they know how to communicate their message. Great principals are the ones, who *expect* to win and lose, and they know from those losses, there will be a lesson learned and they will not forget what the lesson taught them.

Tony Dungy, the Super Bowl winning football coach and author of The Mentor Leader (2010), believes it is important to reflect about how you are perceived by the people you are leading. He poses an interesting question (and one that you should always keep *in the front* of your mind): *"How does your leadership style need to change so that people will flourish and grow around you?"*

Finally [Grease Spot #79]

Everyone is your friend until you start telling the truth.

Bottom Line

I want to share this Chinese poem that I have on the wall in my office.

> Go to the people.
> Learn from them.
> Love them.
> Start with what they know and
> build on what they have.
> But of the best leaders,
> when their task is accomplished and
> their work is done;
> the people will remark
> "We have done it ourselves"

Lau-tzu's Tau Te Ching, verse 17.
This is a translation by Stephen Mitchell.

References

Agnes, M. E. (2004). Webster's new world dictionary. (4th ed.) Hoboken, NJ: John Wiley & Sons.

Are Zero Tolerance Policies Effective in Schools? An evidentiary review and recommendations. *American Psychologist,* December 2008.

Bennis, W. & Goldsmith, J (1994). *Learning to Lead: A Workbook on Becoming a Leader*. Perseus Books.

Bennis, W., Cummings, T. G., & Spreitzer, G. M. (2001). *The Future of Leadership*. San Francisco, CA: John Wiley & Sons, Inc.

Bennis, W. (2003). *On becoming a leader*. New York, New York: Perseus Publishing.

Collins, J. (2001). *Good to great: Why some companies make the leap... and others don't*. New York, NY: Harper Business.

Convey, S. (1989), *Seven habits of highly effective people*. Rosetta Books, NY.

Darling-Hammond, L. (June 14, 2010). Education: How America's commitment to equity will determine our future. *The Nation*.

Dewey, J. *How we think*. (1933). Boston, MA: Heath.

Dungy, T. *The mentor leader*, (2010), Carol Stream, Il: Tyndale Publishers.

Frase, L. & , R., (1990). *School management by wandering around. Lancaster, PA: Technomic Publishing Company, Inc.*

Fullan, M. (1991) *Change forces*. New York, NY: Routledge-Falmer.

Goleman, D., Richard, B., & McKee, A. (2002). *Primal leadership*. Boston, MA: Harvard Business School Press.

Gordon, S. P. (2004). *Professional development for school improvement: Empowering learning communities*. Boston, MA: Allyn & Bacon.

Hirsh, S. & Killion, J. (Mar 2009). *Phi Delta Kappan*, Vol. 90, Issue 7.

Horner, R.H., Sugar, G., Horner, H.F. (2000). A school-wide approach to school discipline. The School Administrator. February, 20-23.

Ingersoll. R. (2003), *Who controls teachers' work? Power and accountability in America's schools*. Boston, MA: Harvard University Press.

Kaniuka, T. (2009) NCLB, school-based instructional policy and decision-making: A proposed research agenda. College Student Journal.

Kouzes, J. M. & Posner, B.Z. (2007). *The leadership challenge*. San Francisco, CA: John Wiley & Sons, Inc.

Krause, D. (2005). *The art of war for executives* New York, NY: Penguin Group Inc.

Lunenberg, Fred C. & Ornstein, Allan C. (2008). *Educational administration: Concepts and Practices*. Belmont, CA: Thomson Higher Education.

Lustig, M. W., & Koester, J. (2003). *Intercultural competence: Interpersonal communication across cultures*. Boston, MA: Allyn and Bacon.

Machiavelli, Niccolo, (1513). *The prince*. New York, NY: Dover Publications, Inc.

Marion, R. (2005). *Leadership in education: Organizational theory for the practitioner*. Long Grove, Il: Merrill/Prentice-Hall.

Maxwell, J. (2003). *Developing the leader within you*. Nashville, TN: Thomas Nelson, Inc.

Murphy, D & Sternberg, D. (2011). Technology: Making sure it is not the third rail in the classroom

Northouse, P., (2007). *Leadership: Theory and practice*. Thousand Oaks, CA: Sage Publications.

Robins, Stephen P. & Judge, Timothy A. (2009). *Organizational behavior*, Prentice Hall.

Samovar, L.S, & Porter, R. E. (1982). *Intercultural communication: A reader*. 6th Edition. Belmont, CA: Wadsworth.

Schon, DA. (1983). *The reflective practitioner: How professionals think in action*. New York: Basic Books.

Skiba, Russell J. (2000). *Zero Tolerance, Zero Evidence: An analysis of school disciplinary practice policy research report #SRS2.*

Welch, J. (2005). *Leadership excellence*, 22(6).

Zero Tolerance is Zero Intelligence. Delaware Liberal. 06 October 2009. http://www.delawareliberal.net/2009/10/06/zero-tolerance-is-zero-intelligence.